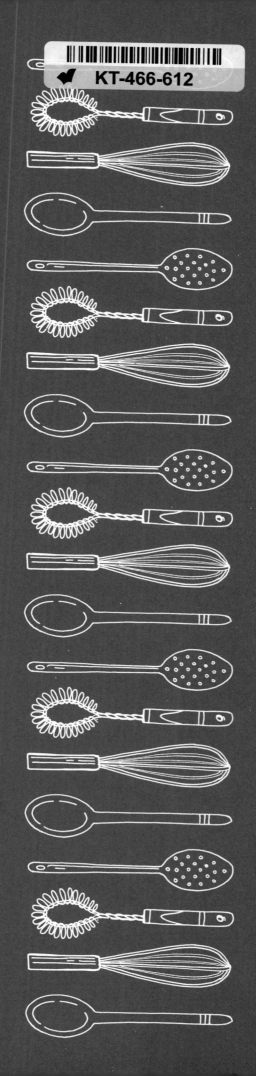

THE AGE-DEFYING COOKBOOK

THE AGE-DEFYING COOKBOOK

OVER 50 RECIPES PACKED WITH YOUTH-ENHANCING NUTRIENTS

CONTRIBUTING EDITOR DR MARIOS KYRIAZIS

LORENZ BOOKS

CUP
10/01

First published by Lorenz Books in 2001

© Anness Publishing Limited 2001

Lorenz Books is an imprint of
Anness Publishing Limited
Hermes House
88–89 Blackfriars Road
London SE1 8HA

Published in the USA by Lorenz Books, Anness Publishing Inc.
27 West 20th Street, New York, NY 10011

www.lorenzbooks.com

This edition distributed in Canada by Raincoast Books
9050 Shaughnessy Street, Vancouver, British Columbia V6P 6E5

Publisher: Joanna Lorenz
Managing Editor: Linda Fraser
Project Editor: Susannah Blake
Editorial Reader: Hayley Kerr
Introduction: Dr Marios Kyriazis
Recipes: Catherine Atkinson, Oona van den Berg, Jacqueline Clarke, Trish Davies,
Joanna Farrow, Christine France, Yasuko Fukuoka, Nicola Graimes, Deh-Ta Hsiung,
Sara Lewis, Lesley Mackley and Sallie Morris
Photography: Janine Hosegood, with additional pictures by Steve Baxter, Nicky Dowey,
Gus Filgate, Ian Garlick, Dave Jordan, Don Last, William Lingwood, Liz McAulay,
Craig Robertson and Tony Stone Images (pp6, 8b, 9t, 9b and 21)
Designer: Ian Sandom
Nutritional Analysis: Clare Brain
Indexer: Dawn Butcher

1 3 5 7 9 10 8 6 4 2

The diets and information in this book are not intended to replace advice from a qualified
practitioner, doctor or dietician. Always consult your health practitioner before adopting
any of the suggestions in this book.

NOTES
For all recipes, quantities are given in both metric and imperial measures
and, where appropriate, measures are also given in standard cups and spoons.
Follow one set, but not a mixture, because they are not interchangeable.

Standard spoon and cup measures are level.
1 tsp = 5ml, 1 tbsp = 15ml, 1 cup = 250ml/8fl oz

Australian standard tablespoons are 20ml. Australian readers should
use 3 tsp in place of 1 tbsp for measuring small quantities.

Medium (US large) eggs are used unless otherwise stated.

All bracketed terms are intended for American readers.

CONTENTS

INTRODUCTION

As we begin to understand more about the mysteries of ageing, we become better able to find ways of delaying it and reducing its impact. New research results and exciting discoveries about the ageing process are constantly coming to light, stimulating the interest of all those who want to live a longer and healthier life. This book offers a glimpse into the intricacies of the ageing process, the consequences it holds for our bodies and ways in which the effects can be avoided.

THE AGEING PROCESS

Ageing is, of course, a natural part of life and traditionally scientists say that it has four characteristics:

- It is universal: it affects everybody and everything.
- It is intrinsic: it is in our genes. We can change the way we live and affect other external factors but, at present, we cannot affect our genetic make-up.
- It is progressive: it cannot be stopped and it is irreversible.
- It is deleterious: it causes worsening of health and body function.

Cutting-edge research shows that some of these characteristics may not actually hold true as was previously believed. For example, we may soon be able to manipulate and change our genes. In fact, during cloning experiments, scientists have managed to fool nature and reset the cellular ageing clock to zero. Treatment with telomerase, a special enzyme that strengthens and grooms our genetic material, may prove another effective gene-buster.

Also, the ageing process may not be that irreversible after all. Age-related damage undeniably happens, but there are some instances in which it can actually be reversed, and others in which it can at least be halted or slowed down. Some of the age-related damage that can be reversed is described below:

- As we age, we normally lose muscle tissue. Treatment with growth hormone can reverse this loss, albeit only temporarily.
- Bone tissue weakens and becomes fragile and porous with age, resulting in osteoporosis. Treatment with oestrogen and certain other special drugs reverses the increase of porosity and brittleness of bones.
- Our memory gradually becomes more sluggish as a result of increasing age. This is a normal process that affects everybody as they grow older. However, experiments have shown that performing mental exercises, or taking supplements such as ginkgo biloba, can actually help reverse this sluggishness, making the older participants in the experiments perform as well as their younger counterparts.

As for ageing causing a worsening of health and body functions, this almost certainly used to be true. However, doctors and scientists are making use of all available research in order to offer new therapies and reduce age-related damage to the body. We are now in a position to reduce the deleterious effects of ageing by following a scientifically endorsed nutritional regime, adopting a healthy lifestyle, practising anti-ageing meditation and taking physical exercise.

Left: Ageing is a natural part of life but new research shows that it may be possible to slow ageing and stay younger longer.

THE CAUSES OF AGEING

There are many different theories as to why we age, all of which help us to see how nutrients and supplements can be used to fight ageing.

Free Radicals

One of the most well-known theories of ageing is the free radical one. Free radicals are harmful by-products of our metabolism, which cause several types of damage to our body tissues, resulting in ageing and age-related disease. For example, free radical damage has been implicated in causing a range of problems, including:
• arthritis
• hardening of the arteries, which can result in stroke or heart attack
• wrinkles
• eye problems
• liver and kidney damage.

This theory is quite interesting because it allows us to do something about our own ageing. Avoid or eliminate free radicals and you will reduce ageing. Free radical toxins can be reduced by following the correct diet and by avoiding pollution, cigarette smoke, excessive alcohol and stress, toxic chemicals and lack of (or excessive) exercise.

Poor Immunity

Another theory blames the immune system for causing ageing. It is our immune system that is in charge of protecting us from outside intruders such as viruses, bacteria and toxins. If our immune system is below par, we can become susceptible to frequent infections – colds, thrush, cold sores and cystitis, for example – or even to the onset of cancer.

To counteract the effects of poor immunity, scientists suggest a whole programme of lifestyle changes, which can include clean, natural living, stress prevention, detoxing and cleansing, together with healthy eating, regular moderate exercise and the taking of suitable supplements.

Above: Taking plenty of regular exercise, adopting a healthy lifestyle, and taking suitable supplements will help you to stay young in both mind and body.

Hormone Imbalance

There are many other theories that try to explain what causes ageing. One that is gaining in popularity is "the neuro-endocrine theory", which considers the prime cause of ageing to be hormone imbalance. To counteract the effects, supporters of this theory suggest hormonal therapies which aim to elevate hormones that are low and reduce those that are high. The main hormones used in this respect are growth hormone and DHEA (De-Hydro-Epi-Androsterone). Hormones that go progressively out of control are:

The thyroid hormone – Low levels of this hormone may result in tiredness, loss of energy, constipation, and feeling cold. Certain scientists believe that almost 40 per cent of all adults have low levels of thyroid hormone, which do not always show up in blood tests.

Melatonin – Low melatonin levels may cause symptoms similar to jet lag: confusion, irritability, depression, sleep disturbance or constipation.

Cortisol – Excessive amounts of this hormone are related to stress. It is normal for the body to have high levels of cortisol for a short period after a stressful event, but if levels remain elevated for longer it can cause various problems, including loss of muscle tissue, weight gain, high blood pressure and diabetes.

Growth hormone – Low levels of growth hormone can cause an increase in body fat, loss of muscle, problems with memory and the immune system, and thin skin.

Sexual and regulating hormones – Levels of other hormones, such as the sexual ones – oestrogen, progesterone and testosterone – and those hormones that are responsible for regulating other hormones in the body are liable to become unbalanced with age.

THE PHYSICAL EFFECTS OF AGEING

Whatever the cause of ageing, our bodies change and develop throughout life. The following explains how the body changes with age, and what to expect during the different life stages.

Age 25–35

Everything is at its peak during this period. Muscle tissue, brain function and sexual prowess are as good as they will ever be. Nature wants us to be in top condition during this stage to ensure the survival of the species – by having children and bringing them up to be healthy in order that they themselves develop into strong and healthy adults. Most people during this life stage have lots of social contacts, a fact which minimizes age-related health problems in years to come. However, your body is still affected by the ageing process from the inside, so you need to plan ahead in order to reduce any future problems. Go for regular check-ups, invest in a good choice of health supplements and keep your mind and body active.

Age 36–45

This is the time when real ageing begins. Muscle tissue gradually weakens, the skin becomes damaged, resulting in the onset of wrinkles and age spots, and the immune system begins to become less efficient. Having said that, there are benefits to be enjoyed as well. People say that their life becomes more enjoyable, they understand things better, they generally have fewer financial worries and they no longer have the problems they had when they were younger. Social and mental factors become important at this stage. Those who have a positive mental attitude, and actually look forward to the future, have the best chances of maintaining their health.

Regarding the brain, there are some changes, such as loss of brain cells, which may affect memory. Cutting-edge thinking, however, supports the view that contrary to what has been believed for generations, the brain cells (neurones) may be able to reproduce, grow and multiply. This is a good thing for those who worry about failing memory in years to come.

Above: Those who look towards the future positively are more likely to enjoy good health as they grow older.

Age 46–55

Biologically, the body is aged. This is the time of the menopause in women and a similar condition in men, known as the andropause. Hormone levels decline in the body, causing further muscle wasting, white hair, increase of body fat and loss of body water. Sexual problems may appear, but these are mostly related to the menopause or the andropause and are treatable.

At this stage in life you should not necessarily accept that you are getting old. Many of the problems of ageing can be reduced or even eliminated altogether. Look at ageing positively – as just a different and more interesting life stage – although you will still need to make some extra effort to look after your body and mind. The need for appropriate supplements becomes more important for many people of this age.

Left: Between the ages of 36 and 45, real ageing begins. However, despite the negative effects of this process, many people find that they start to enjoy life more.

Regular health check-ups to detect potentially serious conditions before they are allowed to develop into real problems are also necessary.

Age 55–plus

Depending on your earlier lifestyle, you can feel as young and healthy as a 35-year-old at this stage in your life. The changes to the body mentioned above may worsen and others may appear for the first time, such as loss of hearing, visual problems and an increased likelihood of heart disease, arthritis or cancer.

However, this matters little to those who maintain a healthy lifestyle, and to those who have strong social bonds, who remain active and think of ageing as an asset rather than a burden. People who believe that ageing is only a case for "doom and gloom" are those who are socially aged. Those who regard their current age as the best yet and meet life's challenges positively are more likely to come to terms with the consequences of ageing.

Above: Those who look after their health early in life are likely to reap the benefits and feel fitter as they get older.

Below: Having a positive mental attitude and enjoying life to the full plays an essential part in feeling younger longer.

HOW TO SLOW DOWN PHYSICAL AGEING

As you go through life, there are a number of simple steps that you can take to reduce the speed of physical ageing. These key steps become more important as you grow older, but it's never too early to start.

• Eat a healthy, balanced diet and follow a healthy lifestyle.

• Invest in a good choice of anti-ageing health supplements.

• Keep your mind and body active.

• Adopt a positive mental attitude towards ageing.

• Work at building and maintaining good relationships and strong social networks and bonds.

• Go for regular health check-ups to detect any potentially serious health conditions.

AGE-DEFYING NUTRIENTS

There are several factors that can accelerate ageing and many others that can slow it down. An important factor is nutrition. Some nutrients accelerate ageing, others defy it. As we have seen, many scientists believe the process of ageing to be greatly affected by free radicals. These can be neutralized by our body's own defences, one of which is referred to as "free-radical scavenging". We have our own supply of antioxidants, the chemicals which counteract free radicals, and these patrol our bloodstream and tissues, seeking free radicals to neutralize.

ANTIOXIDANTS

There are many different types of antioxidants and so-called "free-radical scavengers", which include:
• vitamins C and E
• betacarotene
• grape seed extract
• lycopene
• lutein and zeaxanthin
• polyphenols and catechins.

To really take full advantage of the neutralizing qualities of antioxidants, we need to know how we can boost our supplies of these useful age-defying chemicals. Some people eat them, others swallow them in tablet form and others take them in the form of an injection. The best approach is to consume them in the food we eat. There are many foods that contain the antioxidants mentioned above.

Vitamins and Betacarotene
Rich sources of vitamin C are citrus fruits and certain tropical fruits such as papaya, kiwi fruits and mangoes. You can find high concentrations of vitamin E in nuts and sunflower seeds, as well as green tea, wheatgerm and liver. Betacarotene is found in yellow or deep-coloured fruits, including mangoes, and vegetables such as carrots, kale and spinach.

Above: Grape seed extract is a powerful antioxidant that can be taken either in a supplement or by chewing the seeds found in fresh grapes.

Grape Seed Extract
This is a very strong free radical scavenging antioxidant, particularly if prepared from the seeds of white and green grapes. It is also said to help keep capillaries and connective tissue in good condition.

Many people chew the seeds when eating grapes to gain the maximum benefits from this valuable anti-ageing nutrient. However, some people find this unpalatable. Grape seed extract is also available in tablet form, which can be found in most health food shops.

Left: Oranges, mangoes, kiwi fruits, sunflower seeds and kale are all rich sources of the age-defying vitamins that can help to neutralize harmful free radicals, which can damage the body.

Lycopene

Another great antioxidant, lycopene, is found in tomatoes. Surprisingly, raw tomatoes are not a particularly rich source of this chemical. Cooked tomatoes, tomato ketchup or tomato sauce are much better sources.

Lutein and Zeaxanthin

These phytochemicals are found in several fruits and vegetables, but the best sources are blueberries and bilberries. Lutein and zeaxanthin are used primarily to fight ageing of the eye, but also have a role to play in cancer prevention and in protecting the brain against the effects of ageing.

Polyphenols, including Catechins

These come from many sources but mainly from green tea. This is an ideal drink because it deals with many age-related problems before they appear.

Above: Unlike most nutrients, the powerful antioxidant lycopene can actually be found in richer supplies in cooked tomatoes than in fresh, raw ones.

Above: Blueberries are rich in lutein and zeaxanthin, which are said to protect the eyes and brain against ageing and to protect the body against cancer.

Above: Always try to choose organic foods because produce contaminated with pesticides and other harmful chemicals can accelerate the production of free radicals, which can damage body tissue and speed up the ageing process.

ORGANIC FOODS

Food polluted with pesticides or other chemicals accelerates the production of free radicals that can, in turn, accelerate the ageing process. Try to choose organically grown food to safeguard against future health problems. There are many scientific papers endorsing organic foods.

Our modern way of living also exposes us to many other stresses and poisons. To neutralize these, we need extra supplies of beneficial nutrients found in organic food. However, to gain sufficient amounts of these beneficial chemicals, we would need to eat a great deal. For example, to obtain beneficial amounts of phyto-nutrients we would need to eat 2.5kg/5½lb of green salad a day. This being impractical, some experts believe the next best thing is to take these nutrients in supplement form.

OTHER AGE-DEFYING NUTRIENTS

As well as antioxidants, there are a number of other essential anti-ageing nutrients that can help to slow down, and reduce the effects of, the biological processes of ageing. Many of these nutrients are also antioxidants but have other essential age-defying properties.

Isoflavones

These antioxidant nutrients help to regulate and balance levels of oestrogen and other hormones in the body. Soya beans and soya products are a rich source if isoflavones, and there are also thousands of different isoflavones found in many plants and plant products.

Vitamins B_6, B_{12} and Folate

All of these affect methylation, which is an essential process that keeps our DNA and proteins in good condition. These nutrients are also believed to help protect the heart and brain from age-related damage. Oily fish, liver and green vegetables are good sources of these nutrients.

Above: Soya beans and soya products, such as beancurd (tofu), soya milk and tempeh, are anti-ageing superfoods, containing co-enzyme Q_{10} and hormone-balancing isoflavones.

Left: Drinking plenty of pure water and herbal teas is essential if you want to stay looking and feeling younger.

FLUIDS

Maintaining adequate hydration is one of the main concerns of many anti-ageing devotees. Everyone needs to drink at least eight glasses of fluids a day, preferably water, green tea or herbal teas. If you live in a hot, dry country you need to drink even more than eight glasses a day, to avoid premature ageing. To mention an example, one of the features of skin ageing is dehydration, and many skin specialists advise not only the use of rehydrating creams but also maintaining adequate fluid intake. Remember, drinks containing alcohol and caffeine have a de-hydrating effect on your system.

Above: Oily fish, such as mackerel and trout, are excellent sources of vitamins B_6 and B_{12}, which help to keep body protein and DNA in good condition.

Vitamin K

This is increasingly being recognized as an excellent anti-ageing vitamin. It is believed to help reduce the risk of osteoporosis, improve bone health, strengthen the gums and reduce the risk of heart disease. Sources include leafy vegetables such as broccoli and Brussels sprouts, liver, yogurt, beans, soya and lean red meat.

Carnosine

This is a special amino acid present in brain, muscle and eye tissues. It helps to fight the process of glycosylation, which is the dangerous coupling of sugar molecules to our valuable body protein, causing widespread destruction during ageing.

Carnosine is also an antioxidant, and it helps the body fight toxic material from pollution or from internal chemical reactions. This remarkable nutrient is found in lean red meat and chicken, and is also marketed in capsule form.

Co-enzyme Q_{10}

This really is an anti-ageing super-nutrient. The list of benefits of this essential antioxidant is unbelievably long. Co-enzyme Q_{10} is also called ubiquinone, indicating that it is found in almost any part of the body. It is a natural substance that is produced in the body. Unfortunately, its natural production in the body begins to decline early in life, around the age of 20. This tends to leave the body deficient in co-enzyme Q_{10} later in middle age.

It is an ideal nutrient for helping in the prevention of many diseases and problems related to ageing. Among many things, it is believed to lower blood pressure, boost the immune system, protect the brain and eyes from damage and help prevent heart disease.

Co-enzyme Q_{10} fights the ageing process at the mitochondrial level (mitochondria are the power-houses of our cells, where all the energy needed for efficient body function is produced). This valuable nutrient can be found in oily fish such as trout, sardines, mackerel and whitebait, nuts, soya beans and soya products, such as beancurd (tofu), tempeh and soya milk.

CALORIE RESTRICTION

Limiting the number of calories we consume may help us live longer. In many laboratory experiments, scientists have found that feeding animals with about 30 per cent fewer calories than usual makes the animal live a longer, healthier life. Some believe that the results of research may apply to humans and suggest that we eat less to achieve longer life.

One reason why a calorie-restricted diet could affect lifespan is that it may reduce the amount of harmful free radicals in the body. Another reason may be that calorie-restricted diets reduce the amount of sugar and insulin imbalance, frequently found in older individuals. Whatever the reason, many people find it quite acceptable to reduce the number of calories they consume, without compromising on the quality of the diet, or on its enjoyment factor, in an attempt to extend their life.

Above: Natural live yogurt provides a good supply of vitamin K, which is believed to contribute to bone health, prevent osteo-porosis, strengthen gums and reduce the risk of heart disease.

NUTRITIONAL SUPPLEMENTS

All of the nutrients mentioned are also available as supplements, from health-food stores. There tends to be great confusion about the preparation processes, correct dosage and value for money regarding nutritional supplements; however, as a general rule, remember that you get what you pay for. Here are some supplements that work to slow down or reverse the ageing process.

Acetyl-carnitine

This supplement is believed to protect the brain against age-related damage and facilitates energy production within the cells of the whole body. It also protects the mitochondria against damage. Recent research has suggested that acetyl-carnitine may also have a role to play in helping to reduce the side-effects of Alzheimer's disease in some sufferers.

Alpha Lipoic Acid

This is a very strong antioxidant, which helps in the metabolism of glucose and boosts the effectiveness of other antioxidants such as vitamins E and C and co-enzyme Q_{10}. It plays a role in the prevention of cancer, poor immunity and inflammation.

DHEA (De-Hydro-Epi-Androsterone)

You may have heard of this anti-ageing hormone, which is used and misused by millions of people across the world. If used correctly, it may prevent obesity, brain problems and arthritis among other conditions. It boosts the function of the immune system and may even prevent certain types of cancer. If abused it can contribute to a series of side-effects, the worst of which is prostate cancer.

Growth Hormone

During ageing, our supplies of this hormone, which is necessary for our growth and development, decrease. Supplementation with growth hormone injections was found to reverse several of the signs of ageing, such as weak muscle tissue, thin skin and fragile bones. Due to the expense, as well as the potentially serious side-effects, many people use supplements that stimulate their own supplies of growth hormone from the brain. Such supplements are the amino acids arginine (which is sometimes also used to prevent heart disease and impotence), ornithine, lysine and many others. These are collectively called secretagogues because they facilitate secretion.

Melatonin

Those who suffer from difficulty in sleeping, a problem that often increases with age, may find melatonin useful. Some researchers believe that

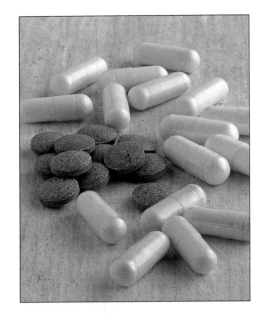

Above: (Clockwise from top left) Acetyl, carnitine, lysine, alpha lipoic acid and ginkgo biloba are a few of the many supplements that can help to slow ageing.

melatonin supplements also prolong lifespan but this has not been proven beyond doubt in humans. Melatonin regulates our body clocks and it is responsible for the sleep/wake cycle.

Nootropics

Also called "brain boosters", these are a large family of different chemicals that protect, nourish and stimulate the brain, not only against ageing but also for maximum performance during everyday life. Examples include drugs such as piracetam, centrophenoxine and hydergine, as well as nutrients such as ginkgo biloba, vinpocetine, bacoba and phosphatidyl serine. Some of the nootropic drugs are not available in certain countries but the rules change constantly, and many devotees obtain supplies via the Internet.

ALCOHOL

Drinking one or two glasses of red wine a day can be beneficial to health, as red wine contains nutrients such as resveratrol, a powerful heart protector with anti-ageing properties. However, it is not advisable to drink more than two glasses a day.

SEEK PROFESSIONAL ADVICE

Always consult a qualified health practitioner before taking supplements or embarking on any course of treatment.

NUTRIENTS THAT ACCELERATE AGEING

In your effort to consume food and nutrients that will reduce the effects of ageing, you need to remember two things. As well as choosing foods that can help to delay the ageing process, you should also try to avoid foods that can actually accelerate age-related damage to the body.

SUGAR

There is no escaping the fact that sugar is one of the key nutrients that cause ageing. Molecules of glucose react with the proteins in our bodies and with our DNA during a process called glycosylation. The result of this dangerous liaison is the destruction of our valuable genetic material and our body constituents.

Stress causes an increase in the amount of sugar in our blood and this is one of the reasons why excessive stress is bad for us. Too much sugar in the blood causes an increase of insulin which, again, is harmful in the long term, because insulin increases the levels of "bad" fats in the blood.

So, one of the first major steps you need to take in your fight against ageing is to shun sugar, completely if possible. Also avoid eating too many simple carbohydrates such as flour, white bread, pitta bread and white rice (although strangely, brown rice is an ideal anti-ageing food).

GOOD AND BAD FATS

Cholesterol comes in two forms: HDL, the "good" form, and LDL, the "bad" form. Ideally, you need to concentrate your efforts on consuming foods that will reduce levels of LDL, such as olive oil, rapeseed oil, avocados and nuts. CLA (conjugated linoleic acid) is a "good" fat found in sunflower oil, safflower oil, milk and lean red meat, that is thought to lower levels of cholesterol. Avoid foods that have the effect of raising LDL, such as processed foods, crisps, biscuits or too many dairy products.

Being overweight is a proven minus point for those who want to defy ageing. Fortunately, another benefit of CLA is that it may help to dissolve fat, and allow it to be used by the muscles for boosting energy.

HOMOCYSTEINE

This harmful amino acid is the latest buzzword from the world of heart disease prevention. Homocysteine is thought to cause havoc in our body, increasing the risk of heart disease, cancer, dementia and many other problems that can be age-related. In order to reduce its production, choose foods high in vitamin B_{12}, including liver and oily fish such as trout and salmon, and high in folate, found in green leafy vegetables, such as cabbage, kale and Brussels sprouts.

Above: Sugar and refined carbohydrates, such as white bread, are the worst culprits when it comes to foods that age the body, so try to avoid them whenever possible.

FOODS AND SUPPLEMENTS THAT CAN WORSEN AGE-RELATED PROBLEMS

• Gout is made worse by eating too much protein, drinking too much alcohol and by being overweight.
• Indigestion is caused by fatty, fried food, tea, coffee and alcohol.
• High blood pressure may worsen with excessive intake of salt, eating too much fatty food and overeating in general.
• Migraines can sometimes be made worse by eating certain foods, such as cheese, chocolate, nuts and many others.
• Ageing can also be accelerated by taking extra iron supplements, as iron speeds up the production of free radicals. It is best taken only in food form, for example red meat. Take iron supplements only if your doctor advises you to do so.

COMBATING AGEING DISEASES

Following the right nutritional regime is like taking the path to good health. Although it can often seem like an uphill struggle, it can also be very enjoyable – and the result will always be worthwhile. Doctors, nutritionists and researchers from all over the world are increasingly realizing that many, if not all, human diseases are influenced, one way or another, by what we eat.

Left: Calcium is essential for strong bones and can be found in milk, sesame seeds, almonds, whitebait and yogurt.

Diseases related to ageing, like other illnesses, can be at least partly treated or prevented by choosing our food and drink wisely. However, correct nutrition is only part of the story. A disease can only be prevented or treated effectively when a whole combination of nutrients, lifestyle changes, suitable treatments and medication is used.

Some of the diseases related to ageing can be difficult to treat once they are established. However, if you take the necessary steps early in life when you are still considered young, then the likelihood of your developing certain diseases can be greatly reduced. Some experts recommend that ageing prevention should begin as early as the teenage years in order to cut the risk of premature ageing to a minimum.

OSTEOPOROSIS
This is one of the most typical age-related illnesses. Nutrition in this case has proved invaluable in preventing the condition. Fortifying our bodies with plenty of calcium during the early years of life – teenage and early adulthood – can reduce the risk of developing the disease in later years. Foods that contain rich supplies of this valuable nutrient include sesame seeds, almonds, beans, beancurd (tofu) and dairy products, such as milk, cheese and yogurt. Other foods that offer good supplies of calcium include sprats, whitebait and sardines, particularly when their bones are eaten as well.

As well as calcium, vitamin D is also necessary for strong bones. Extra vitamin D can be obtained by eating more oily fish and fortified breakfast cereals, or by taking it in tablet form. Sunlight is essential in boosting vitamin D supplies in the body. (Remember, always protect your skin against ageing from harmful UV rays by using a high protection sun cream.) Osteoporosis may also be prevented with natural plant oestrogens which are derived from a variety of sources, but mainly from soya beans and soya products, such as beancurd (tofu).

Normally our diet contains certain minerals which are indispensable in preventing osteoporosis, such as boron and zinc, but some women prefer to take these in tablet form as an extra protection against the disease.

DISEASES OF THE JOINTS
Arthritis is another disease partly related to age. It may be difficult to prevent arthritis with nutrition alone, but some sensible steps for reducing the symptoms of the disease include:
• Avoiding fried foods.
• Reducing your intake of animal fat to a minimum.
• Obtaining your protein supplies from pulses, skimmed milk, nuts or beans.
• Ensuring you include the "good" fats, omega-3 fatty acids, which are thought to be ideal for arthritis sufferers. These are abundant in fish such as halibut, haddock, cod and salmon.
• Avoiding toxins such as cigarette smoke and too much alcohol.

Once established, arthritis is treated with a great variety of therapies, but the main nutritional supplements used are glucosamine and chondroitin. These two substances are the raw materials that are necessary for good joint health. Some people believe that eating animal cartilage, which contains these two vital chemicals, safeguards against the risk of developing arthritis in the future. This idea has not been proven in scientific experiments but research continues.

BRAIN FUNCTION AND MEMORY PROBLEMS

Brain and memory problems can affect many people as they grow old. Some scientists believe that fortifying our brains through nutrition early in life can minimize the risk of brain problems in later life. Fish is at the top of the list of brain foods and is probably the best known. Then come soya products, fruit and green vegetables and the different vitamins in the B group, which are to be found in kidneys, liver and yogurt.

Nutritional supplements such as co-enzyme Q_{10}, ginkgo biloba and phosphatidyl serine are also used by millions of people worldwide, and

Below: Nutrients found in oily fish such as trout, halibut and salmon are excellent for both brain and bone health.

Above: Antioxidant nutrients found in strawberries, soya beans, tomatoes and spinach protect the eyes against damage.

research supports their use as general brain boosting supplements. Newer "smart" nutrients that are appearing on the scene are bacoba monniera, which is the extract of the Indian brahmi plant, and huperzine, which is an extract from the Chinese herb Huperzia serrata. These are, in fact, plants that have been used since ancient times, but they have only recently been rediscovered in the West.

AGE-RELATED EYE CONDITIONS

Two potentially serious age-related eye problems are cataracts and macular degeneration. These eye diseases are thought to have a variety of causes, but some scientists believe that they can both be prevented.

Consuming suitable antioxidants from early in life may help reduce the risk of these eye problems in the future. Go for the standard antioxidant vitamins A, C and E, but also add the chemicals that are currently the most fashionable, which are worth their weight in gold: lutein and zeaxanthin. These are thought to protect the eye from the inside, reducing the free radical damage to the parts of the eye that are affected by age. Lutein and zeaxanthin are found in blueberries, bilberries, strawberries and kale.

Aspirin may also play a part in preventing cataracts because it reduces inflammation and free radical damage in the eye. Isoflavones (from soya) and lycopene (from tomatoes) are also a good bet for eye protection due to their antioxidant properties.

Another main cause of eye damage is UV radiation from the sun, which can damage the delicate eye tissues. Always wear sunglasses when going out in the sun, even if it is not a very bright day, to protect your eye tissues from this avoidable damage.

MINOR AGE-RELATED HEALTH PROBLEMS

As well as the more serious diseases related to ageing, there are a number of other physical changes and health problems. Though these problems are rarely serious, most people would prefer to reduce or avoid them as they grow older.

Infections and Poor Immunity

A poor immunity is a hallmark of premature ageing. Nutrients that can help in boosting the function of the immune system, thus making it easier for our bodies to fight infections, are antioxidants (particularly vitamins E and A), fish oils and the mineral zinc, which is found in seafood, mushrooms, grains, seeds and nuts. Echinacea is a herbal supplement that can be used on a short-term basis during some mild infections such as colds. Avoid stress, fatty foods and smoking, all of which depress the immune system, and take moderate exercise, which is known to boost immunity.

Above: Dandelion and cranberry juice can be used to help fight urinary-tract infections.

Sexual Problems

Depending on your age, you may need extra supplies of sexual hormones such as progesterone or testosterone. These are usually available in tablet, injection or skin patch form. Phytoestrogens can be obtained from soya beans and soya products and there are any number of supplements that can be used in order to boost libido and sexual enjoyment. These are: the amino acid arginine, muira puama, ginseng, ginkgo biloba, yohimbine and choline. Vitamin E is also reputed to increase sexual stamina. Good supplies of this vitamin can be found in wheatgerm, nuts and seeds.

Menopause

Obtain your phytoestrogens from chickpeas and other pulses, as well as soya, arrowroot, nuts and clover, in tablet form. Isoflavones can reduce many unpleasant symptoms and are found in red wine, grains and deep-coloured vegetables, or may be taken in tablet form. Supplements include both dong quai and CLA (conjugated linoleic acid), which is believed to help reduce the risk of breast cancer.

Prostate Problems

Overweight men tend to be more at risk from developing disease of the prostate. Increase your intake of rye and eat plenty of fruit and vegetables, particularly tomatoes which contain the prostate-loving chemical lycopene. Soya beans and products may also help boost your supplies of essential plant hormones, necessary for excellent prostate health.

Wrinkles and Skin

To prevent premature skin ageing, you should use sun screen lotions religiously throughout life to protect your skin from the UV radiation of the sun. Avoid packaged foods that contain sodium and saturated acids, as both are bad for the skin. Follow a cleansing and detoxing programme. Wheatgrass and spirulina contain plant chemicals which help tone up the skin. Also consider vitamins, selenium, other antioxidants and organic linseed (flax) oil, which is a rich source of the all-important omega-3 fatty acids. Some women use progesterone creams or aloe vera creams with some success.

Above: Phytoestrogens found in lentils and walnuts can help alleviate the sometimes unpleasant symptoms of the menopause.

Above: Wheatgrass juice and wheatgrass supplements are well-known detoxifiers. They also contain valuable plant chemicals that help to tone up the skin.

Hair Loss

The health of your hair often reflects the health of your body. However, there are many different causes of hair loss, which tends to affect men more than women, but some scientists believe that the most common problems are related to nutrition.

The amino acid lysine may help, and this is available in lean red meat or in tablet form. Eat foods that are high in iron, such as red meat, but don't take extra iron supplements because these may worsen free radical damage to the skin. The B vitamins have also been indicated as playing an important role in hair health. Ginkgo biloba is a very effective stimulant of the circulation in general, and it may help to invigorate sluggish blood flow to the hair follicles.

You could also try gently massaging your scalp using rosemary, sage or lavender oil, to nourish the hair and invigorate the scalp and hair follicles. Don't wash your hair too frequently as this destroys the natural protective oils of the scalp.

Varicose Veins

Regular exercise and nutrition both play a part in the prevention of varicose veins. A high-fibre diet is thought to help, as are bioflavonoids found in blackcurrants, apricots and grapes. However, this has not been scientifically proven. There are several herbal remedies for strengthening the veins. The most widely used is horse chestnut, which contains natural plant astringents. Massaging the affected area with cypress oil or creams containing marigold may also help.

Nutritional supplements are lecithin, mainly from soya, and antioxidant nutrients in general. Hazel and cotu cola (also called Centella asiatica) are two of the latest additions to our armoury, sometimes combined with the rare flavonoids hesperidin and diosmin. These are available in capsule form from certain health-food stores. Centella is, in fact, an ancient remedy, but recent research on its skin-healing effects has been very promising. Avoid standing for too long and don't cross your legs when sitting because this may restrict the blood flow in your veins.

Above: Massaging the scalp with rosemary, sage and lavender oils is thought to help reduce hair loss and encourage growth.

Above: Having an Ayurvedic massage with sesame oil or taking lemon balm or ginger supplements are all thought to help combat the unpleasant symptoms of vertigo.

Vertigo

This condition occurs when the sense of balance is disturbed. Symptoms include a whirling sensation and giddiness. Herbal supplements for vertigo include ginkgo biloba and vinpocetine, which is the extract of the periwinkle plant. These two supplements help restore normal blood flow within the inner ear, which is responsible for maintaining the correct balance of the body, and should relieve dizziness. Some people find that ginkgo biloba is more effective than vinpocetine. Lemon balm or ginger supplements are also used to combat the symptoms of vertigo. Avoid caffeine, found in tea, coffee, cola drinks and chocolate.

You can also take advantage of a specialist Ayurvedic (ancient Indian) treatment, which involves massage with sesame oil or having the oil dripped on to your head. There are also specific Ayurvedic anti-vertigo head exercises, which may be learned from specialist medical centres.

DETOXING AND CLEANSING

Detoxification as a way of defying premature ageing is rapidly gaining support. Our body performs its own natural detox and cleansing processes every day, but every now and then it just needs a bit of encouragement. During a detox programme you need to choose fresh, organic foods and drinks that have been produced without the use of chemicals. It is important to realize that a detox programme needs preparation for one or two days beforehand and should not be repeated very frequently. A suitable time for detoxing would be over a weekend or holiday.

FASTING

If performed properly, fasting gives the body a break from the daily overload of unhealthy chemicals. Liquid fasting, involving organic vegetable and fruit juices, is ideal. Fasting does not mean starving. It means avoiding certain foods, for short periods only, without compromising on the nutritional quality. If you are on medication or suffer from any illnesses, it is best to ask your doctor before fasting.

IDEAL DETOXING FOODS

Choose organic produce whenever possible, and wash all fruit and vegetables thoroughly before use. Source your food where you know there is a rapid turnover of produce, so that freshness is guaranteed. Include the following in your programme.

- citrus fruit such as grapefruit, satsumas, lemons and oranges
- grapes and cherries
- dried (unsulphured) fruit, particularly apricots, pineapple, raisins and sultanas
- any fresh, raw, and organically grown vegetables
- grains, pulses and seeds.

A ONE-DAY DETOX

7 a.m. Cup of hot water with a few drops of elderflower juice. Meditation and stretching exercises.
8 a.m. Breakfast of freshly blended fruits mixed with orange juice.
9 a.m. One of the following: massage, reflexology, pilates exercise sequence or aromatherapy.
11 a.m. A piece of fruit and a glass of water.

Above: Giving your skin a good brush will help to invigorate circulation.

12 p.m. Lunch of home-made vegetable soup.
2 p.m. Chat with a close friend spending some time talking about issues that interest you. Allow yourself enough time to reflect on the conversation afterwards.
3 p.m. Spend some time looking after your body. For example, give yourself a revitalizing face mask, a hair and nail treatment or similar.
4 p.m. Brisk walk, a swim or home exercises such as tai chi or qigong (chi kung). Large glass of fruit juice and mineral water.
6 p.m. Cup of herbal tea.
7 p.m. Fresh, raw vegetable salad. Spend the evening reading, relaxing, and having a bath, and give yourself a good rub with a loofah (or similar) to revitalize the circulation.

COLONIC IRRIGATION

This technique uses purified water to cleanse the bowel and flush out toxins. Colonic irrigation once every few weeks may provide benefits, but mainstream medicine has not yet given it the final seal of approval.

Above: Organic flageolet beans, grapes, oranges and onions are all excellent foods to eat while detoxing as they encourage the system to cleanse itself.

AGE-DEFYING EXERCISE

Physical exercise can be both very good or very bad for ageing. Many people wrongly believe that more is better. However, that is not always the case. Excessive exercise can accelerate the effects of ageing in our bodies, while mild to moderate exercise can have great benefits.

MILD TO MODERATE EXERCISE

A sensible level of exercise can be achieved through activities such as brisk walking for 20 to 30 minutes a day, swimming, cycling, home exercises, gym workouts lasting up to 30 minutes once or twice a week, gardening and an active lifestyle in general, such as walking instead of driving, or using the stairs instead of the lift. This type of exercise:

- Increases HDL, which is the "good" cholesterol.
- Decreases triglycerides, the so-called "bad" fats.
- Strengthens the muscles and helps the tissues absorb oxygen better.
- Improves immunity.
- Reduces the amount of insulin and glucose in the body, which is good not only for diabetics but for everyone who wants to avoid premature ageing.
- Helps to clear the brain and the thought processes.
- Reduces the risk of high blood pressure, heart disease, heart attack and stroke.
- Strengthens the bones and reduces the risk of osteoporosis.

EXCESSIVE EXERCISE

Over-exercising should be avoided as it can do more harm than good when it comes to ageing. For example, taking over 45 minutes of vigorous exercise at a time, such as in the gym, weight lifting, swimming or jogging:

- Increases the production of free radicals in the body.
- Increases the levels of the stress hormone cortisol which, in turn, accelerates several of the effects of ageing such as glucose damage (glycosylation) and kidney damage.
- Reduces the amount of "energy", as perceived by Oriental medicine.

The Chinese believe that we are born with an allocated amount of energy, and when we use this up we age and die. Excessive exercise uses up this energy quickly, causing premature ageing. Exercises that help preserve this vital energy, such as qigong (chi kung) and tai chi, are believed to help us live longer.

ORIENTAL EXERCISES

Exercises such as yoga, tai chi and qigong (chi kung) are ideal age-defying activities. One of the reasons is that, as mentioned above, they help the body to work out without expending too much energy. In fact, qigong in particular helps the body actually to build up its energy supplies.

It is possible to get a fairly basic understanding of these exercises from a book, but it is best to learn from a qualified teacher. Certain exercises are better suited to an anti-ageing regime than others. In yoga for example, the head-standing posture increases the blood flow to the brain, which helps stimulate the secretion of hormones, reduces the effects of gravity on the face muscles and strengthens the sense of balance. Overall, the best anti-ageing postures are found within the several thousand positions used in qigong. This is a combination of elegant movements, breathing exercises and meditation so, like yoga and tai chi, it is ideal for maximizing the health of body and mind.

Above: Tai chi is a perfect age-defying exercise as it gives your body a workout without expending too much vital energy.

BODY AND MIND

It is not enough just to follow a good diet and take regular exercise in the hope that you will defy the ageing process. The correct way to fight ageing should also deal with the effects of ageing on the whole individual. Physical ageing can also be combated using the mind. The link between body and mind is very strong, and there is a growing body of research supporting this.

Experiments show that recalling happy events can increase certain beneficial constituents of the immune system (immunoglobulins) and thus protect the body against infections. In another recent experiment, praying was shown to reduce the effects of heart disease. It is therefore important to engage in regular positive thinking, age-defying meditation and general mental training.

COMPLEMENTARY MEDICINE

During our fight against ageing we need all the help we can get, and it is here that complementary medicine comes into its own, offering several treatments that are relevant to ageing. By using a combination of orthodox and complementary treatments, we maximize our chances of living a long, healthy and enjoyable life.

Acupuncture

This Chinese method of healing relieves symptoms by inserting needles in specified points under the skin. It is usually helpful in treating certain age-related health conditions, such as pain from arthritis, cancer and osteoporosis. Acupuncture can also be helpful in reducing the effects of the menopause, depression and anxiety.

Ayurvedic Medicine

The main aim of this ancient Indian system of medicine is to improve health and longevity. Its main focus is nutrition, supported primarily by the use of herbs, massage and aromatic oils, but there are many complementary branches as well, which treat the patient as a whole being.

Modern medicine is rediscovering the benefits of ancient Ayurvedic medicine, particularly those that have relevance to ageing. Ayurvedic herbs called *rasayanas* aim to strengthen the link between body and mind, and include many different preparations. One of these is called *ashwaghanda* (Withania somnifera), which is believed to be one of the best age-defying Oriental herbs. It is used to treat general weakness, arthritis, chest diseases and sexual problems, as well as depression.

Breathing Therapy

During breathing therapy, you will learn how to use the correct muscles of the chest and abdomen for making full use of the oxygen taken with each breath. Practitioners also try to reduce the frequency of breathing, from the normal 12, down to five or six cycles a minute. This is believed to reduce the formation of harmful free radicals that can damage the body, and thus reduces age-related damage.

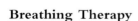

Left: Breathing therapy teaches you to use chest and abdomen muscles correctly, helping you to make full use of the oxygen taken in each breath.

Above: Reduce the ageing potential of stress by creating a relaxing environment, using candles, aromatherapy oils and gentle music to help clear the mind.

Music Therapy

Many of us use music therapy without even realizing it. Listening to music has many benefits for our health. It relaxes the brain, clears the thought processes and stimulates the immune system to be more efficient. Music therapy is also ideal for stimulating our memories and for recalling long-forgotten incidents and events from our memory banks.

Magnetism

The benefits of magnetism are slowly being unravelled by researchers. With regard to ageing in particular, magnetic therapy is used to reduce the pain of arthritis, strengthen the bones, alleviate sleeping problems and relieve nervous tension. Some researchers also believe that it helps slow down ageing within our cells, but others say that more research evidence is required before they will be convinced.

Hydrotherapy

Water has been used therapeutically for many centuries. Today, several different treatments are used: hot or cold baths, hosing with cold water, exercises in water and alternating hot and cold showers to the lower body to reduce the symptoms of cystitis. Hydrotherapy is a natural treatment but it has to be used wisely to reap the full benefits. It can be used both for prevention of illnesses and for treatment.

Homeopathy

This treatment prescribes small doses of drugs that produce similar symptoms to those of the disease itself. Almost any disease can be treated using homeopathic remedies. Age-related health problems in particular, such as menopause problems as well as arthritis and muscle aches and pains, can benefit from this type of therapy. As in the case of acupuncture, this is a complementary therapy that is mainly effective when a disease has already become established, rather than as a preventative treatment.

Herbalism

The use of herbs to maximize health is very popular at present. There are hundreds of different herbs that have health benefits in ageing. These include:

- Lavender, which reduces muscle aches, raises the spirits and helps calm the mind. Lavender oil can be used externally, but fresh lavender can also be used in teas and tinctures.
- Arnica, which is used for improving blood circulation and in the healing of skin ulcers or wounds.
- Black cohosh, which is used for relieving menopause problems and has also been used to prevent PMS.
- Cat's claw, which is helpful both in revitalizing the immune system and reducing inflammation.
- Dandelion, which is recommended for gall-bladder and liver problems. It also facilitates the elimination of toxins from the kidneys and is a very nutritionally rich herb.
- Rosemary, which is said to stimulate the nervous and circulatory systems.

Below: Herbalism extolls the virtues of herbs, such as lavender, arnica and cat's claw, which are thought to slow down and reduce the effects of ageing.

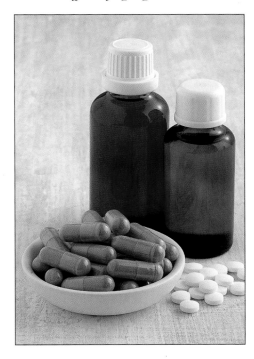

REJUVENATING JUICES

Freshly squeezed fruit and vegetable juices are the perfect way to get a dose of age-defying nutrients. Juices should be drunk within 15 minutes of being made to get the full benefits of their youth-enhancing vitamins, minerals and phytochemicals. As well as providing valuable nutrients, they can also act as powerful detoxifiers, which is important in any anti-ageing regime. Fight free radicals with a glass of antioxidant Sunburst or cleanse your system with a shot of Green Leaves.

Pink Vitality

This high-energy drink is rich in antioxidants and is good for breakfast.

INGREDIENTS

Serves 1

1 peach or nectarine
225g/8oz/2 cups
   strawberries
30ml/2 tbsp lemon juice

--- NUTRITION NOTES ---

Per portion:

Energy	99kcals/416kJ
Protein	2.9g
Fat, total	0.4g
saturated fat	0g
Carbohydrate	22.2g
of which sugars	22.2g
Fibre	4.1g

1 Cut the peach or nectarine into quarters around the stone (pit) and pull the fruit apart. Pull out the stone and cut the flesh into rough chunks, then hull the strawberries. Juice the peach or nectarine and strawberries, using a juicer, or blend for a thicker juice. Stir in the lemon juice.

Antioxidant Express

This will shield you from free radicals all day.

INGREDIENTS

Serves 1

1 papaya
1 mango
½ cantaloupe melon
90g/3½oz white grapes

--- NUTRITION NOTES ---

Per portion:

Energy	226kcals/951kJ
Protein	3.2g
Fat, total	0.7g
saturated fat	0g
Carbohydrate	55.4g
of which sugars	54.9g
Fibre	9.9g

1 Halve and skin the papaya, then remove the seeds and cut into rough slices. Peel the mango and cut the flesh from the stone.

2 Remove the melon seeds with a spoon. Slice the flesh away from the skin, then cut into rough chunks. Juice all the fruit.

Power Booster

Summer Tonic

Give your system an extra boost with this cleansing drink.

INGREDIENTS

Serves 1
2 apples
1 large carrot
50g/2oz cooked beetroot (beet) in natural juice
90g/3½oz white grapes
1cm/½in piece fresh root ginger

1 Quarter the apples and top and tail the carrot. Juice the fruit, vegetables and fresh root ginger.

— NUTRITION NOTES —

Per portion:

Energy	176kcals/740kJ
Protein	2.6g
Fat, total	0.5g
saturated fat	0.1g
Carbohydrate	42.9g
of which sugars	42.9g
Fibre	6.3g

— HEALTH BENEFITS —

Beetroot is one of the most effective liver-cleansing vegetables. It is a very good detoxifier and laxative and also provides plenty of antioxidants.

Try this tonic whenever your energy is low.

INGREDIENTS

Serves 1
5cm/2in piece cucumber
3 large vine-ripened tomatoes
½ Little Gem (Bibb) lettuce
1 small garlic clove
small handful of fresh parsley, stalks included
15ml/1 tbsp lemon juice

1 Peel and chop the cucumber. Halve the tomatoes and lettuce. Juice all the ingredients together.

— NUTRITION NOTES —

Per portion:

Energy	59kcals/248kJ
Protein	2.7g
Fat, total	1.3g
saturated fat	0.4g
Carbohydrate	9.9g
of which sugars	9.9g
Fibre	3.5g

— HEALTH BENEFITS —

Although a large part of lettuce is made up of water, it also contains many essential nutrients, including beta-carotene, iron and folic acid.

Green Leaves

This juice will boost
your brain energy.

INGREDIENTS

Serves 1
1 apple
150g/5oz white grapes
small handful of fresh
   coriander (cilantro)
25g/1oz watercress
15ml/1 tbsp lime juice

1 Quarter the apple. Juice
the fruit, coriander and
watercress, then stir in the
lime juice.

— NUTRITION NOTES —

Per portion:

Energy	143kcals/589kJ
Protein	1.9g
Fat, total	0.6g
saturated fat	0.1g
Carbohydrate	35g
of which sugars	35g
Fibre	3.3g

— HEALTH BENEFITS —

Grapes are one of the most
effective detoxifiers and are
excellent for treating skin,
liver and kidney disorders.

Red Protector

This dark red juice will
help boost immunity.

INGREDIENTS

Serves 1
½ small red cabbage
½ fennel bulb
2 apples
15ml/1 tbsp freshly squeezed
   lemon juice

1 Roughly slice the red
cabbage and fennel, and
quarter the apples. Juice the
vegetables and fruit, then stir
in the lemon juice.

— NUTRITION NOTES —

Per portion:

Energy	143kcals/589kJ
Protein	1.9g
Fat, total	0.6g
saturated fat	0.1g
Carbohydrate	35g
of which sugars	35g
Fibre	3.3g

— HEALTH BENEFITS —

Fennel is a well-known natural
diuretic and raw cabbage has
potent antibacterial properties.

Energizer

This juice is rich in anti-
ageing phytochemicals.

INGREDIENTS

Serves 1
3 carrots
25g/1oz young spinach
115g/4oz cooked beetroot
   (beet) in natural juice
2 celery sticks

1 Top and tail the carrots, then
juice all the vegetables.

— NUTRITION NOTES —

Per portion:

Energy	117kcals/493kJ
Protein	4.7g
Fat, total	0.9g
saturated fat	0.2g
Carbohydrate	23.8g
of which sugars	23.5g
Fibre	7.1g

— HEALTH BENEFITS —

Carrots are another key detox
vegetable. Not only do they
cleanse, nourish and stimulate
the body, but they contain a
rich supply of antioxidants.

Morning Glory

This combination makes
a quick antioxidant-
packed breakfast.

INGREDIENTS

Serves 1
3 carrots
1 apple
1 orange

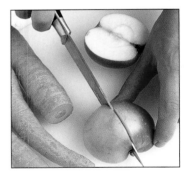

1 Top and tail the carrots,
then quarter the apple.
Peel the orange and cut into
rough segments. Juice the
carrots and fruit.

— NUTRITION NOTES —

Per portion:

Energy	173kcals/729kJ
Protein	2.8g
Fat, total	1.2g
saturated fat	0.2g
Carbohydrate	40g
of which sugars	39.3g
Fibre	9g

— HEALTH BENEFITS —

Natural fruit sugars will help
provide a boost of energy.

Virgin Mary

This refreshing tomato drink will replenish your levels of lycopene, an essential plant chemical for both men and women.

INGREDIENTS

Serves 2
250ml/8fl oz/1 cup chilled
   tomato juice
5ml/1 tsp Worcestershire sauce
few drops of Tabasco sauce
juice of ½ lemon
pinch of celery salt
salt and ground white or black pepper
2–3 spring onions (scallions), shredded,
   to garnish
ice cubes and 2 celery sticks, to serve

1 Pour the chilled tomato juice into a large jug (pitcher).

2 Add the Worcestershire sauce and stir well to ensure the flavours are thoroughly combined.

3 Add a few drops of Tabasco sauce and the lemon juice. Taste and season with celery salt, salt and black or white pepper, if necessary. Serve over ice cubes, with celery sticks for stirring.

— NUTRITION NOTES —	
Per portion:	
Energy	9kcals/41kJ
Protein	0.5g
Fat, total	0g
saturated fat	0g
Carbohydrate	2g
of which sugars	2g
Fibre	0.4g

Tropical Refresher

The therapeutic and anti-ageing properties of lime are well-known. Whenever you need a pick-me-up, this zesty juice is sure to provide the spark you need.

INGREDIENTS

Serves 4
2 pineapples
juice of 2 limes
475ml/16fl oz/2 cups still
   mineral water
about 15ml/1 tbsp honey
ice cubes, to serve

1 Peel the pineapples and chop, removing the core and "eyes". Put the flesh in a food processor or blender and add the lime juice and half the mineral water.

2 Purée to a smooth pulp. Stop the machine and scrape the mixture from the side of the food processor or blender once or twice during processing.

3 Place a strainer over a large bowl. Pour and scrape the pineapple pulp into the strainer, then press it through with the back of a wooden spoon to extract the juice.

4 Pour the sieved liquid into a large jug (pitcher), cover and chill in the refrigerator for about 1 hour.

5 Stir in the remaining mineral water to dilute the mixture and add honey to taste. Serve with ice.

NUTRITION NOTES	
Per portion:	
Energy	69kcals/296kJ
Protein	0.5g
Fat, total	0.3g
saturated fat	0g
Carbohydrate	17.3g
of which sugars	17.3g
Fibre	1.5g

Citrus Spring

A good source of vitamin C, this refreshing drink will neutralize a substantial amount of harmful free radicals, protecting your tissues against age-related damage.

INGREDIENTS

Serves 1
2 oranges
1 lemon
5ml/1 tsp granulated sugar
75ml/5 tbsp water
slices of orange and lemon,
   to decorate
crushed ice, to serve

VARIATION

This same principle can be used to obtain nutrients from other fruits.

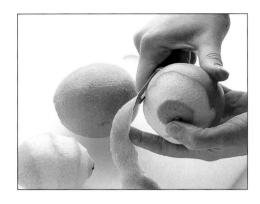

1 Wash the oranges and lemon and then pare off the rinds with a sharp knife, leaving the bitter white pith behind. Remove the pith from the fruit and discard it.

2 Put the orange and lemon rind in a heavy pan, with the sugar and water. Heat gently over a low heat and stir gently until the sugar has dissolved.

3 Remove the pan from the heat and press the orange and lemon rind against the sides of the pan to release all their oils. Cover the pan and cool. Remove and discard the rind.

4 Purée the oranges and lemon and sweeten by adding the cooled citrus syrup over the fruit pulp. Leave aside for 2–3 hours for the flavours to infuse.

5 Strain the fruit, pressing to extract as much of the juice as possible.

6 Pour into a tall glass filled with crushed ice and decorate with slices of orange and lemon.

NUTRITION NOTES

Per portion:
Energy	37kcals/159kJ
Protein	0.16g
Fat, total	0.1g
saturated fat	0g
Carbohydrate	9.1g
of which sugars	9.1g
Fibre	0.1g

Sunburst

A refreshing and tasty drink, packed with antioxidants. The combination of carrots and strawberries is really unusual, but deadly to any free radicals.

INGREDIENTS

Serves 2

1 green eating apple, cored and chopped
3 carrots, peeled and chopped
1 mango, peeled and stoned (pitted)
150ml/¼ pint/⅔ cup freshly squeezed orange juice, chilled
6 strawberries, hulled
slice of orange, to decorate
ice cubes, to serve

1 Place the apple, carrots and mango in a food processor or blender and process the mixture to a pulp.

2 Add the orange juice and hulled strawberries and process again.

3 If liked, strain the pulp through a strainer, pressing out all the juice with the back of a wooden spoon. Discard any pulp left in the sieve.

4 Pour the juice into tumblers filled with ice cubes and serve immediately, decorated with a slice of orange.

VARIATION

Use 4 or 5 fresh apricots in place of the mango for a slightly different flavour, or make a delicious breakfast smoothie by blending in some natural (plain) yogurt.

NUTRITION NOTES

Per portion:
Energy	125kcals/529kJ
Protein	1.9g
Fat, total	0.7g
saturated fat	0.2g
Carbohydrate	29.6g
of which sugars	29g
Fibre	5.1g

Date Dynamo

Dates have been used as a healthy and uplifting food for millennia. They are packed full of healthy, rejuvenating energy and contain natural plant chemicals which can help to revitalize the body and the metabolism.

INGREDIENTS

Serves 1
1 litre/1¾ pints/4 cups water
225g/8oz dates
2 limes
ice cubes, to serve

1 Pour the water into a pan and heat until warm. Pour into a bowl, add the dates and leave to soak for 4 hours.

2 Place a strainer over a clean bowl. Pour the dates and their soaking water into the strainer, then press the pulp through the sieve with the back of a wooden spoon, leaving the stones behind. Discard the stones.

3 Juice the limes and stir the juice into the date mixture in the bowl. Pour the juice into a jug (pitcher) and chill thoroughly before serving in tumblers filled with ice.

HEALTH BENEFITS

Dates are packed with natural fruit sugars, which provide plenty of energy but are much kinder to the body than refined sugars. As well as providing energy, dates are a good source of calcium, which is needed for healthy bones. Limes are rich in antioxidant vitamin C, which can help to neutralize the harmful free radicals found in the body.

NUTRITION NOTES

Per portion:

Energy	54kcals/230kJ
Protein	0.7g
Fat, total	0.1g
saturated fat	0g
Carbohydrate	13.6g
of which sugars	13.6g
Fibre	0.8g

Melon Pick-me-up

This refreshing drink, containing vitamin C and B vitamins, is very uplifting and will provide valuable support to your age-defying programme.

INGREDIENTS

Serves 4
1 watermelon
1 litre/1¾ pints/4 cups chilled water
juice of 2 limes
clear honey, to taste
ice cubes, to serve

1 Cut off the watermelon skin, discard the shiny black seeds and cut the flesh into chunks.

2 Place the watermelon chunks in a large bowl, pour in the chilled water and allow the mixture to stand for 10 minutes.

3 Transfer the soaked watermelon chunks to a large strainer set over a mixing bowl. Using a wooden spoon, press gently on the fruit to extract all the liquid.

4 Add the lime juice and any soaking water to the melon mixture and stir, then sweeten to taste with honey.

5 Pour the juice into a jug (pitcher), add ice cubes and stir. Serve immediately in glasses.

HEALTH BENEFITS

Antioxidant vitamin C, which is found in lime juice, will help to fight free radicals that can damage the body.

NUTRITION NOTES

Per portion:	
Energy	25kcals/109kJ
Protein	0.1g
Fat, total	0g
saturated fat	0g
Carbohydrate	6.6g
of which sugars	6.6g
Fibre	0g

Soups and Starters

The dishes in this chapter are all made with wholesome, low-fat ingredients, specially chosen for their age-defying properties. A bowl of Hot and Sour Soup with Tofu will provide your body with a healthy dose of co-enzyme Q_{10} to help prevent heart disease, brain failure and other age-related problems. If you're after antioxidants, make a meal of Roasted Butternut Squash Soup, or start off with spicy Mango Salsa before choosing a delicious anti-ageing main course.

Hot and Sour Soup with Tofu

INGREDIENTS

Serves 6

4–6 Chinese dried mushrooms
2–3 small pieces of wood ear and a few
  golden needles (lily buds) (optional)
115g/4oz pork tenderloin, cut into
  fine strips
45ml/3 tbsp cornflour
  (cornstarch)
150ml/¼ pint/⅔ cup water
15–30ml/1–2 tbsp sunflower oil
1 small onion, finely chopped
1.5 litres/2½ pints/6¼ cups good
  quality chicken stock
150g/5oz drained fresh firm beancurd
  (tofu), diced
60ml/4 tbsp rice vinegar
15ml/1 tbsp light soy sauce
1 egg, beaten
5ml/1 tsp sesame oil
salt and ground white or black pepper
2–3 spring onions (scallions), shredded,
  to garnish

1 Place the dried mushrooms in a bowl, with the wood ear and the golden needles (lily buds), if using. Add enough warm water to cover and leave to soak for about 30 minutes.

2 Drain the mushrooms, reserving the soaking water. Cut off and discard the mushroom stems and slice the caps finely. Trim away any tough stems from the wood ears, then chop them finely. Using kitchen string, tie the golden needles into a bundle.

3 Dust the strips of pork tenderloin with some of the cornflour; mix the remaining cornflour to a smooth paste with the water.

4 Heat the oil in a wok or pan and fry the onion until soft. Increase the heat and fry the pork until it changes colour. Add the stock, mushrooms, soaking water, and wood ears and golden needles, if using. Bring to a boil, then simmer for 15 minutes.

5 Discard the golden needles, if necessary, then lower the heat and stir in the cornflour paste to thicken. Add the beancurd (tofu), vinegar, soy sauce, and salt and pepper.

6 Bring the soup to just below boiling point, then drizzle in the beaten egg by letting it drop from a whisk so that it forms threads in the soup. Stir in the sesame oil and serve at once, garnished with spring onion shreds.

NUTRITION NOTES	
Per portion:	
Energy	154kcals/647kJ
Protein	7.3g
Fat, total	7.8g
saturated fat	1.5g
Carbohydrate	14.7g
of which sugars	0.6g
Fibre	0.2g

Chicken, Avocado and Chickpea Soup

This soup is packed with age-defying nutrients found in lean chicken, chickpeas and avocados, and is so substantial it can be enjoyed for lunch or dinner on its own.

INGREDIENTS

Serves 6

1.5 litres/2½ pints/6¼ cups
  chicken stock
½ chipotle chilli, seeded
2 skinless, boneless chicken breasts
1 medium avocado
4 spring onions (scallions),
  finely sliced
400g/14oz can chickpeas,
  drained
salt and freshly ground black pepper

1 Pour the chicken stock into a large pan and add the chilli. Bring to the boil, add the whole chicken breasts, then lower the heat and allow to simmer for about 10 minutes or until the chicken is cooked.

2 Remove the pan from the heat and lift out the chicken breasts with a slotted spoon. Leave to cool a little.

3 Using two forks, shred the chicken into small pieces. Set the shredded chicken aside.

4 Pour the chicken stock into a blender or food processor and add the chilli. Process the mixture until smooth, then return to the pan.

5 Cut the avocado in half, remove the skin and stone (pit), then slice the flesh into 2cm/¾in pieces. Add it to the stock, with the spring onions and chickpeas. Return the shredded chicken to the pan, with salt and black pepper to taste, and heat gently. When the soup is heated through, spoon into warmed bowls and serve.

HEALTH BENEFITS

Lean chicken is a good source of the all-round anti-ageing nutrient carnosine, which helps the body to fight toxins. Chickpeas replenish the body's supplies of flavonoids, while avocados are a good source of vitamin E and B vitamins.

NUTRITION NOTES

Per portion:

Energy	182kcals/765kJ
Protein	16.3g
Fat, total	8.3g
saturated fat	1.7g
Carbohydrate	11.4g
of which sugars	0.6g
Fibre	3.7g

Borscht

This invigorating Russian soup is rich in antioxidant betacarotene, which helps fight the ageing process.

INGREDIENTS

Serves 4-6
900g/2lb uncooked beetroot
  (beets), peeled
2 carrots, peeled
2 celery sticks
50g/2oz/¼ cup butter
2 onions, sliced
2 garlic cloves, crushed
4 tomatoes, peeled, seeded and chopped
1 bay leaf
1 large parsley sprig
2 cloves
4 whole peppercorns
1.2 litres/2 pints/5 cups chicken stock
150ml/¼ pint/⅔ cup liquid from
  pickled beetroot (beets)
salt and freshly ground black pepper
natural (plain) yogurt, to serve
dill sprigs, to garnish (optional)

1 Use a sharp knife to cut the uncooked beetroot, carrots and celery into fairly thick strips.

2 Melt the butter in a large heavy pan. Add the sliced onions and cook over a low heat for about 5 minutes, until transparent, stirring occasionally. Add the prepared strips of beetroot, carrot and celery and continue to cook over a low heat for a further 5 minutes. Stir occasionally to ensure the vegetables do not stick or burn.

3 Add the garlic and chopped tomatoes to the pan and cook, stirring, for 2 minutes more.

4 Place the bay leaf, parsley, cloves and peppercorns in a piece of muslin and tie with string.

5 Add the muslin bag to the pan with the stock. Bring to the boil, reduce the heat, cover and simmer for 1¼ hours, or until the vegetables are very tender. Discard the bag. Stir in the liquid from the pickled beetroot and season. Bring to the boil. Ladle into bowls and serve with natural yogurt garnished with dill sprigs, if liked.

NUTRITION NOTES	
Per portion:	
Energy	140kcals/589kJ
Protein	3.8g
Fat, total	6g
saturated fat	3.7g
Carbohydrate	19.2g
of which sugars	17g
Fibre	4.8g

Sorrel and Spinach Soup

This is another age-defying idea from Russia, with extra fish to top up those much-needed omega-3 fatty acids. These help reduce the risk of heart disease and stroke, while keeping the joints in good condition.

INGREDIENTS

Serves 4

25g/1oz/2 tbsp butter
225g/8oz sorrel, washed and
    stalks removed
225g/8oz young spinach, washed
    and stalks removed
25g/1oz fresh horseradish, grated
750ml/1¼ pints/3 cups apple juice
1 pickled cucumber, finely chopped
45ml/3 tbsp lemon juice
30ml/2 tbsp chopped fresh dill
225g/8oz cooked fish, such as
    pike, perch or salmon, skinned
    and boned
salt and freshly ground black pepper
sprig of dill, to garnish

1 Melt the butter in a large pan. Add the prepared sorrel and spinach leaves and the grated fresh horseradish. Cover the pan and gently cook for 3–4 minutes, or until the sorrel and spinach leaves are wilted.

2 Spoon the cooked spinach and sorrel leaves into a food processor or blender and process to a fine purée. Ladle the purée into a tureen or serving bowl and stir in the apple juice, chopped cucumber, lemon juice and chopped dill.

3 Chop the cooked fish into bite-size pieces. Add to the soup, then season with salt and plenty of ground black pepper. Chill for at least 3 hours before serving, garnished with a sprig of fresh dill.

HEALTH BENEFITS

Leafy green vegetables, such as sorrel and spinach, are rich in betacarotene, which helps to fight free radicals in the body.

NUTRITION NOTES

Per portion:

Energy	186kcals/771kJ
Protein	13.3g
Fat, total	13.7g
saturated fat	4.8g
Carbohydrate	2.8g
of which sugars	2.6g
Fibre	2.5g

Genoese Minestrone

INGREDIENTS

Serves 4-6

1 onion
2 celery sticks
1 large carrot
45ml/3 tbsp olive oil
150g/5oz French (green) beans, cut
    into 5cm/2in pieces
1 courgette (zucchini), thinly sliced
1 potato, cut into 1cm/½in cubes
¼ Savoy cabbage, shredded
1 small aubergine (eggplant), cut into
    1cm/½in cubes
200g/7oz can cannellini beans, drained
    and rinsed
2 Italian plum tomatoes, chopped
1.2 litres/2 pints/5 cups vegetable stock
90g/3½oz dried spaghetti or vermicelli
salt and freshly ground black pepper

For the pesto
about 20 fresh basil leaves
1 garlic clove
10ml/2 tsp pine nuts
15ml/1 tbsp freshly grated Parmesan
15ml/1 tbsp freshly grated Pecorino
30ml/2 tbsp olive oil

1 Chop the onion, celery and carrot finely, either in a food processor or by hand. Heat the olive oil in a large pan, add the chopped vegetables and cook over a low heat, stirring frequently, for 5–7 minutes.

2 Add the French beans, courgette, potato and cabbage to the pan. Cook for 3 minutes, then add the aubergine, cannellini beans and plum tomatoes. Cook for a further 3 minutes.

3 Pour in the stock with salt and pepper to taste. Bring to the boil. Stir, cover and lower the heat. Simmer for 40 minutes, stirring occasionally.

4 Meanwhile, process all the pesto ingredients in a food processor until the mixture forms a smooth sauce, adding 15–45ml/1–3 tbsp water through the feeder tube if necessary.

5 Carefully break the spaghetti or vermicelli into small pieces and add it to the soup. Simmer, stirring frequently, for 5 minutes.

6 Add the pesto sauce and stir it in well, then allow the soup to simmer for a further 2–3 minutes, or until the pasta is *al dente*. Taste for seasoning. Serve the soup hot, in warmed soup plates or bowls.

HEALTH BENEFITS

Tomatoes are an excellent source of the antioxidant lycopene, which becomes abundant when tomatoes are cooked. Cannellini beans provide a valuable dose of B vitamins, which are essential in the battle against ageing.

NUTRITION NOTES

Per portion:

Energy	254kcals/1063kJ
Protein	8.6g
Fat, total	13.1g
saturated fat	2.6g
Carbohydrate	27.6g
of which sugars	7.1g
Fibre	5.2g

Roasted Butternut Squash Soup

The fresh thyme and oregano or marjoram in this nutritious soup have been found to have good anti-ageing properties.

INGREDIENTS

Serves 4–5

2 garlic bulbs, outer papery
 skin removed
75ml/5 tbsp olive oil
a few fresh thyme sprigs
1 large butternut squash, halved
 and seeded
2 onions, chopped
5ml/1 tsp ground coriander
1.2 litres/2 pints/5 cups vegetable or
 chicken stock
30–45ml/2–3 tbsp chopped fresh
 oregano or marjoram
salt and freshly ground black pepper

For the salsa
4 large ripe tomatoes, halved
 and seeded
1 red (bell) pepper, halved and seeded
1 large fresh red chilli, halved
 and seeded
30–45ml/2–3 tbsp extra virgin olive oil
15ml/1 tbsp balsamic vinegar
pinch of caster (superfine) sugar (optional)

1 Preheat the oven to 220°C/425°F/ Gas 7. Place the garlic bulbs on a piece of foil and pour over half the oil. Add the thyme, then fold the foil around the garlic to enclose completely. Place on a baking sheet with the squash and brush the squash with 15ml/1 tbsp of the remaining oil. Add the tomatoes, red pepper and fresh chilli for the salsa.

2 Roast for 25 minutes, then remove the tomatoes, pepper and chilli. Reduce the temperature to 190°C/ 375°F/Gas 5 and cook the squash and garlic for 20–25 minutes more, or until the squash is tender.

3 Heat the remaining oil in a large, heavy pan and cook the onions and ground coriander gently for about 10 minutes, or until softened.

4 Skin the pepper and chilli and process in a food processor or blender with the tomatoes and 30ml/ 2 tbsp olive oil. Stir in the balsamic vinegar and seasoning to taste, adding a pinch of caster sugar, if necessary. Add the remaining oil if you think the salsa needs it.

5 Squeeze the roasted garlic out of its papery skin into the onions and scoop the squash out of its skin, adding it to the pan. Add the stock, 5ml/1 tsp salt and plenty of black pepper. Bring to the boil and simmer for 10 minutes.

6 Stir in half the fresh oregano or marjoram and let the soup cool slightly before processing it in a food processor or blender. If you prefer, press through a fine strainer.

7 Reheat the soup without allowing it to boil, then taste for seasoning before ladling it into warmed bowls. Top each serving with a spoonful of salsa and sprinkle over the remaining chopped oregano or marjoram. Serve the soup immediately.

— NUTRITION NOTES —	
Per portion:	
Energy	146kcals/607kJ
Protein	2.1g
Fat, total	11.5g
saturated fat	1.7g
Carbohydrate	9.5g
of which sugars	6.8g
Fibre	2.8g

Mango Salsa

Our sense of taste dulls with age. This spicy salsa will help to stimulate the tastebuds.

INGREDIENTS

Serves 4
2 fresh red Fresno chillies
2 ripe mangoes
½ white onion
small bunch of coriander (cilantro)
grated rind and juice of 1 lime

1 To peel the chillies, spear them on a long-handled metal skewer and roast them over the flame of a gas burner until the skins blister and darken. Do not let the flesh burn. Alternatively, dry-fry them in a griddle until the skins are scorched.

2 Place the roasted chillies in a strong plastic bag and tie the top to keep the steam in. Set aside for 20 minutes.

3 Meanwhile, put each mango on a board and cut off a thick slice close to the flat side of the stone (pit). Repeat on the other side. Score each slice with criss-cross lines at 1cm/½in intervals, taking care not to cut the skin.

4 Fold the mango halves inside out so the flesh stands proud, in dice. Slice these off the skin into a bowl. Cut off the flesh on each stone (pit), dice and add to the bowl.

— NUTRITION NOTES —	
Per portion:	
Energy	65kcals/276kJ
Protein	1.3g
Fat, total	0.3g
saturated fat	0.1g
Carbohydrate	15.4g
of which sugars	13.8g
Fibre	2.8g

5 Remove the roasted chillies from the bag and carefully peel off the skins. Cut off the stems, then slit the chillies and scrape out the seeds.

6 Chop the white onion and the coriander finely and add them to the mango. Chop the chilli finely and add it to the mixture in the bowl, together with the lime rind and juice. Stir well to mix, then cover and chill for at least 1 hour before serving. Store in the refrigerator for up to 3 days.

Roasted Tomato and Coriander Salsa

This great taste stimulant is also full of antioxidants, which help to neutralize harmful free radicals.

INGREDIENTS

Serves 6 as an accompaniment
500g/1¼lb tomatoes
2 fresh serrano chillies
1 onion
juice of 1 lime
large bunch of coriander (cilantro)
salt

1 Preheat the oven to 200°C/400°F/ Gas 6. Cut the tomatoes into quarters and place them in a roasting tin (pan). Add the chillies. Roast them for 45 minutes–1 hour, until the tomatoes and chillies are charred and softened.

2 Place the roasted chillies in a strong polythene bag. Tie the top to keep the steam in and set aside for 20 minutes. Let the tomatoes cool slightly, then remove the skins and dice the flesh.

3 Chop the onion finely, then place in a bowl and add the lime juice and the chopped tomatoes.

— NUTRITION NOTES —	
Per portion:	
Energy	17kcals/75kJ
Protein	0.7g
Fat, total	0.3g
saturated fat	0.1g
Carbohydrate	3.2g
of which sugars	3.2g
Fibre	1g

4 Peel the chillies. Cut off the stalks, then scrape out the seeds. Chop the chillies roughly and add to the onion mixture. Mix well.

5 Chop the coriander and add most to the salsa. Add salt, cover and chill for 1 hour before serving, sprinkled with the remaining coriander. Store in the refrigerator for up to 1 week.

Roasted Pepper Antipasto

Peppers are used by many longevity devotees. The different colourful peppers are a feast to the eye and to the tastebuds, while the artichoke hearts help to improve the health of the digestive system.

INGREDIENTS

Serves 6

3 red (bell) peppers
2 yellow or orange (bell) peppers
2 green (bell) peppers
50g/2oz/½ cup sun-dried tomatoes in oil, drained
1 garlic clove
30ml/2 tbsp balsamic vinegar
75ml/5 tbsp olive oil
few drops of chilli sauce
4 canned artichoke hearts, drained and sliced
salt and freshly ground black pepper
snipped basil leaves, to garnish

1 Preheat the oven to 200°C/400°F/ Gas 6. Lightly oil a foil-lined baking sheet and place the whole peppers on the foil. Bake for about 45 minutes until beginning to char. Cover with a dish towel and leave to cool for 5 minutes.

2 Slice the sun-dried tomatoes into thin strips. Peel the garlic clove, then thinly slice. Set the prepared tomatoes and garlic aside while you make the dressing.

3 In a small bowl, beat together the vinegar, oil and chilli sauce, then season with a little salt and ground black pepper.

4 Peel and slice the peppers. Mix with the artichokes, tomatoes and garlic. Pour over the dressing and scatter with the snipped basil.

HEALTH BENEFITS

Orange, red and yellow peppers are rich in antioxidant betacarotene, which can help to slow ageing by neutralizing harmful free radicals in the body.

NUTRITION NOTES

Per portion:

Energy	145kcals/601kJ
Protein	2.3g
Fat, total	10.6g
saturated fat	1.6g
Carbohydrate	10.2g
of which sugars	10.1g
Fibre	3.4g

Aubergine and Pepper Spread

Use this healthy spread on bread in place of butter and spice up your snack break. It can also be spread on brown pitta bread or oatmeal bread for a light lunch or with freshly cut crudités for a pre-dinner snack.

INGREDIENTS

Serves 6-8
675g/1½lb aubergines (eggplant), halved lengthways
2 green (bell) peppers, seeded and quartered
45ml/3 tbsp olive oil
2 firm ripe tomatoes, halved, seeded and finely chopped
45ml/3 tbsp chopped fresh parsley or coriander (cilantro)
2 garlic cloves, crushed
30ml/2 tbsp red wine vinegar
lemon juice, to taste
salt and freshly ground black pepper
sprigs of parsley or coriander (cilantro), to garnish
dark rye bread and lemon wedges, to serve

1 Place the aubergines and peppers under a preheated grill (broiler), skin side uppermost, and cook until the skin blisters and chars. Turn the vegetables over and cook for a further 3 minutes. Place in a polythene bag and leave for 10 minutes.

2 Peel away the blackened skin and purée the aubergine and pepper flesh in a food processor or blender.

3 With the motor running, pour the olive oil into the food processor or blender in a slow and steady stream, through the feeder tube until the oil has been fully incorporated.

NUTRITION NOTES	
Per portion:	
Energy	57kcals/238kJ
Protein	1.1g
Fat, total	4.6g
saturated fat	0.7g
Carbohydrate	3.2g
of which sugars	2.9g
Fibre	2.3g

4 Carefully remove the blade and stir in the chopped tomatoes, parsley or coriander, garlic, vinegar and lemon juice. Season to taste, garnish with fresh parsley or coriander and serve with dark rye bread and lemon wedges.

Ceviche with Avocado and Sweet Potato

INGREDIENTS

Serves 6 as a starter

500–675g/1¼–1½lb white fish
  fillets, skinned
1 red onion, thinly sliced
pinch of dried red chilli flakes
grated rind of 1 small lime and juice of
  5 limes
450–500g/1–1¼lb sweet potatoes
75ml/5 tbsp mild olive oil
15–25ml/1–1½ tbsp rice vinegar
2.5ml/½ tsp ground toasted
  cumin seeds
½–1 fresh red or green chilli, seeded
  and finely chopped
1 large or 2 small avocados, peeled,
  stoned (pitted) and sliced
225g/8oz peeled cooked
  prawns (shrimps)
45ml/3 tbsp chopped fresh
  coriander (cilantro)
30ml/2 tbsp chopped roasted peanuts
salt and freshly ground black pepper

1 Cut the fish fillets into strips or chunks. Scatter half the sliced red onion over the base of a glass dish and lay the fish on top. Sprinkle on the dried red chilli flakes and pour in the lime juice.

2 Cover the dish with clear film and chill for 2–3 hours, spooning the lime juice over the fish pieces once or twice. Drain the marinated fish, and discard the onion.

3 Steam or boil the sweet potatoes for 20–25 minutes, or until they are just tender. Peel and slice, or cut into wedges.

4 Place the oil in a bowl and whisk in the rice vinegar, then add the ground toasted cumin seeds and season with salt and freshly ground black pepper. Whisk in the fresh chilli and the grated lime rind.

5 In a glass bowl, mix together the marinated fish, sweet potato wedges, avocado slices, prawns and most of the coriander. Pour over the dressing and toss to coat evenly.

6 Toss in the remaining half of the sliced red onion. Sprinkle the ceviche with the remaining fresh coriander and the chopped roasted peanuts and serve at once.

— COOK'S TIP —

Choose an oily fish, such as mackerel, to get maximum anti-ageing benefits.

— NUTRITION NOTES —

Per portion:
Energy	349kcals/1459kJ
Protein	26g
Fat, total	19.7g
saturated fat	3.4g
Carbohydrate	18.2g
of which sugars	5.5g
Fibre	2.3g

Red Mullet with Raspberry Dressing

Start any main meal with this colourful salad. Red or other dark-coloured vegetables are a standard recommendation by all nutritionists who specialize in longevity, so this dish is perfect for anyone following an age-defying diet.

INGREDIENTS

Serves 4

8 red mullet fillets, scaled
15ml/1 tbsp olive oil
15ml/1 tbsp raspberry vinegar
175g/6oz mixed dark green and red
  salad leaves, such as lamb's lettuce,
  radicchio, oakleaf lettuce and
  rocket (arugula)
salt and freshly ground black pepper

For the raspberry dressing

115g/4oz/¾ cup raspberries, puréed
  and sieved
30ml/2 tbsp raspberry vinegar
60ml/4 tbsp extra virgin olive oil

1 Lay the red mullet fillets in a shallow dish. Whisk together the olive oil and raspberry vinegar, add a pinch of salt and drizzle the mixture over the fish. Cover and leave to marinate for 1 hour.

COOK'S TIP

To make the raspberry purée, whizz the fruit in a food processor or blender, then press it through a sieve (strainer) placed over a bowl to remove the seeds.

2 Meanwhile, whisk together the dressing ingredients in a small bowl and season to taste with salt and freshly ground black pepper.

3 Wash the mixed salad leaves well and pat dry with a clean dish towel, then put them in a large bowl. Pour most of the raspberry dressing over the leaves and toss lightly to combine.

--- NUTRITION NOTES ---

Per portion:

Energy	319kcals/1337kJ
Protein	36.6g
Fat, total	18.4g
saturated fat	2.6g
Carbohydrate	2.1g
of which sugars	2.1g
Fibre	1.1g

4 Heat a ridged grilling pan or frying pan until very hot, put in the red mullet fillets and fry for 2–3 minutes on each side, until just cooked. Cut the fillets diagonally in half to make rough diamond shapes.

5 Arrange a tall heap of salad in the middle of each serving plate. Prop up four red mullet fillet halves on the salad on each plate with the reserved dressing spooned around, and serve.

SALADS

Light and refreshing salads make a great contribution to any age-defying diet. Packed with fresh and lightly cooked fruits and vegetables, this selection of recipes makes use of ingredients that will help to keep you young and healthy. Moroccan Date, Orange and Carrot Salad is packed with the anti-ageing vitamins C and E, while Grilled Pepper Salad will help to neutralize free radicals, stimulate the brain and regulate the digestion.

Seaweed Salad

INGREDIENTS

Serves 4

5g/⅛oz each dried wakame, dried
   arame and dried hijiki seaweeds
about 130g/4½oz enoki mushrooms
2 spring onions (scallions)
a few ice cubes
½ cucumber, cut lengthways
250g/9oz salad leaves

For the marinade

15ml/1 tbsp rice vinegar
6.5ml/1¼ tsp salt

For the dressing

60ml/4 tbsp rice vinegar
7.5ml/1½ tsp toasted sesame oil
15ml/1 tbsp shoyu (ordinary
   soy sauce)
15ml/1 tbsp dashi stock
2.5cm/1in piece fresh root
   ginger, grated

1 Soak the wakame for 10 minutes in one bowl of water, and the arame and hijiki for 30 minutes in another.

2 Trim the hard ends of the enoki stalks, then cut in half and separate the stems. Cut the spring onions into thin 4cm/1½in long strips lengthways. Soak the latter in cold water with a few ice cubes to make them curl up. Drain. Slice the cucumber into thin half-moon shapes.

3 Cook the wakame and enoki in boiling water for 2 minutes, then add the arame and hijiki for just a few seconds. Remove them from the heat immediately. Drain and marinate with vinegar and salt while still warm. Chill in the refrigerator.

4 Mix the ingredients for the dressing in a mixing bowl. Arrange the mixed salad leaves in a large bowl and heap up the cucumber, then add the seaweed and enoki mixture. Decorate with spring onion strips and serve with the dressing.

--- HEALTH BENEFITS ---

The Japanese diet is thought to be a key factor in the nation's famous longevity and low incidence of diseases, such as cancer and heart disease. This salad is a fine example of the traditional Japanese idea of eating: look after your appetite and your health at the same time. Seaweed is a nutritious, alkaline food and rich in fibre. Moreover, it has no calories.

--- NUTRITION NOTES ---

Per portion:

Energy	16kcals/69kJ
Protein	1.2g
Fat, total	0.7g
saturated fat	0.1g
Carbohydrate	1.4g
of which sugars	1.3g
Fibre	1g

Parsley and Rocket Salad

Olive oil and parsley are essential ingredients in any age-defying diet. Crunchy green salads like this one are tasty accompaniments to grilled, lean red meat dishes, providing the body with all-round anti-ageing protection.

INGREDIENTS

Serves 6

1 garlic clove, halved
115g/4oz good white bread, cut into
   1cm/½in thick slices
45ml/3 tbsp olive oil, plus extra for
   shallow frying
75g/3oz rocket (arugula) leaves
75g/3oz baby spinach
25g/1oz flat leaf parsley, leaves only
45ml/3 tbsp salted capers, rinsed
   and dried
40g/1½oz Parmesan cheese, pared
   into shavings

For the dressing

25ml/5 tsp black olive paste
1 garlic clove, finely chopped
5ml/1 tsp Dijon mustard
75ml/5 tbsp olive oil
10ml/2 tsp balsamic vinegar
freshly ground black pepper

1 First make the dressing. Whisk the black olive paste, garlic and mustard together in a bowl. Gradually whisk in the olive oil, then the vinegar. Adjust the seasoning with black pepper – the dressing should already be salty.

NUTRITION NOTES

Per portion:

Energy	219kcals/907kJ
Protein	5.1g
Fat, total	17.9g
saturated fat	3.6g
Carbohydrate	9.9g
of which sugars	0.9g
Fibre	2g

2 Heat the oven to 190°C/375°F/ Gas 5. Rub the halved garlic clove over the bread and cut or tear the slices into bite-size croûtons. Toss them in the oil and place on a small baking sheet. Bake for 10–15 minutes, stirring once, until golden. Cool on kitchen paper.

3 Mix the rocket, spinach and parsley in a large salad bowl.

4 Heat a shallow layer of olive oil in a frying pan. Add the capers and fry briefly until crisp. Scoop out straight away and drain on kitchen paper.

5 Toss the dressing and croûtons into the salad and divide it among six bowls or plates. Scatter the Parmesan shavings and the fried capers over the top and serve immediately.

Orange and Red Onion Salad

Fresh mint always adds a welcome flavour to any salad dish. The cumin seeds and black pepper excite the tastebuds which, in turn, stimulate the brain to secrete health-promoting chemicals.

INGREDIENTS

Serves 7
6 oranges
2 red onions
15ml/1 tbsp cumin seeds
5ml/1 tsp coarsely ground
   black pepper
15ml/1 tbsp chopped fresh mint
90ml/6 tbsp olive oil
salt

To serve
fresh mint sprigs
black olives

1 Slice the oranges thinly, working over a bowl to catch any juice. Then, holding each orange slice in turn over the bowl, cut round with scissors to remove the peel and all of the white pith.

2 Using a sharp knife, slice the red onions thinly and then separate into rings.

3 Arrange the orange and onion slices in layers in a shallow dish, sprinkling each layer with cumin seeds, pepper, mint, olive oil and salt. Pour over the reserved orange juice.

4 Leave the salad to marinate in a cool place for about 2 hours. Just before serving, scatter the salad with the mint sprigs and black olives.

NUTRITION NOTES	
Per portion:	
Energy	177kcals/740kJ
Protein	2.4g
Fat, total	11.4g
saturated fat	1.5g
Carbohydrate	17.8g
of which sugars	16.7g
Fibre	3.5g

Spanish Salad with Capers and Olives

This salad contains many key ingredients for optimal health. Both tomatoes and watercress are particularly useful, while capers are a healthy Mediterranean delicacy.

INGREDIENTS

Serves 4
4 tomatoes
½ cucumber
1 bunch spring onions (scallions)
1 bunch purslane or watercress, washed
8 pimiento-stuffed olives
30ml/2 tbsp drained capers

For the dressing
30ml/2 tbsp red wine vinegar
5ml/1 tsp paprika
2.5ml/½ tsp ground cumin
1 garlic clove, crushed
75ml/5 tbsp olive oil
salt and freshly ground black pepper

1 Peel the tomatoes: place them in a heatproof bowl, add boiling water to cover and leave for 1 minute. Lift out with a slotted spoon and plunge into cold water. Leave for 1 minute, then drain. Slip the skins off the tomatoes and dice the flesh finely. Put in a bowl. Cut the cucumber into dice and add to the tomatoes. Trim and chop half the spring onions, add to the salad and mix lightly.

NUTRITION NOTES	
Per portion:	
Energy	151kcals/626kJ
Protein	1.6g
Fat, total	14.9g
saturated fat	1.5g
Carbohydrate	3g
of which sugars	2.9g
Fibre	1.5g

2 Break the watercress or purslane into small sprigs. Add to the tomato mixture, with the olives and capers.

3 To make the dressing, mix together the red wine vinegar, paprika, cumin and garlic in a bowl. Whisk in the olive oil and add salt and black pepper to taste. Pour over the salad and toss lightly. Serve with the remaining spring onions.

Moroccan Date, Orange and Carrot Salad

Almonds are a brilliant source of vitamin E, which works in unison with vitamin C in this exotic salad, maximizing the health and anti-ageing benefits.

INGREDIENTS

Serves 4
1 Little Gem (Bibb) lettuce
2 carrots, finely grated
2 oranges
115g/4oz fresh dates, stoned (pitted) and cut into eighths, lengthways
25g/1oz/¼ cup toasted whole almonds, chopped
30ml/2 tbsp lemon juice
5ml/1 tsp caster (superfine) sugar
1.5ml/¼ tsp salt
15ml/1 tbsp orange flower water

1 Carefully separate the individual lettuce leaves and arrange them in the bottom of a salad bowl or on individual serving plates.

2 Place the finely grated carrot in a mound on top of the arranged lettuce leaves.

3 Peel and segment the oranges and arrange them around the carrot. Pile the prepared dates on top, then sprinkle the salad with the toasted almond pieces.

4 To make the dressing, mix together the lemon juice, caster sugar, salt and orange flower water in a small bowl. When the mixture is thoroughly combined, sprinkle lightly over the salad and serve immediately.

HEALTH BENEFITS

This salad is packed with valuable antioxidants that can help to neutralize the harmful free radicals in the body. Oranges and lemon juice are packed with vitamin C, carrots provide an excellent source of betacarotene, and the almonds contain a useful supply of vitamin E. Fresh dates are high in fibre and provide the body with plenty of energy.

NUTRITION NOTES

Per portion:

Energy	105kcals/441kJ
Protein	2.8g
Fat, total	3.9g
saturated fat	0.3g
Carbohydrate	15.7g
of which sugars	15.4g
Fibre	3g

Grilled Pepper Salad

This is a very colourful dish, an important fact considering that the eyes are the gateway to a good digestion. Bright and colourful dishes stimulate the brain to optimize the regulation of digestive juices, and also provide essential antioxidants.

INGREDIENTS

Serves 4

8 green, yellow and/or orange
  (bell) peppers
1 garlic clove, crushed
75ml/5 tbsp olive oil
60ml/4 tbsp wine vinegar
4 tomatoes, sliced
1 red onion, thinly sliced
freshly ground black pepper
sprigs of fresh coriander (cilantro),
  to garnish

1 Cut the peppers into quarters, discarding the cores, seeds and tops. Place under a preheated grill (broiler), skin side uppermost, and cook until the skin chars and blisters.

NUTRITION NOTES

Per portion:

Energy	204kcals/846kJ
Protein	2.6g
Fat, total	14.8g
saturated fat	2.2g
Carbohydrate	16g
of which sugars	15.1g
Fibre	4.1g

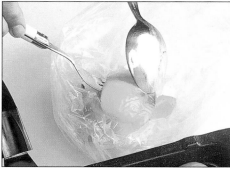

2 Place the peppers in a polythene bag and set aside for about 15 minutes to let their skins loosen.

COOK'S TIP

For an interesting alternative, try using long sweet peppers in this recipe as they produce a slightly different flavour.

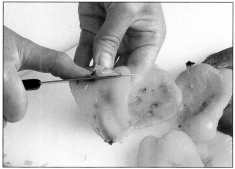

3 Remove the peppers from the bag and scrape off the skins using a sharp knife.

4 Blend together the garlic, olive oil and vinegar. Arrange the peppers, tomatoes and onion on four serving plates and pour over the garlic dressing. Season, garnish with sprigs of coriander and serve.

Grilled Leek and Fennel Salad

Full of freshness, this tempting salad provides useful quantities of fennel and tomatoes, fighting ageing on all fronts.

INGREDIENTS

Serves 6 as a starter

675g/1½lb leeks
2 large fennel bulbs
120ml/4fl oz/½ cup extra virgin
   olive oil
2 shallots, chopped
50ml/2fl oz/¼ cup dry white wine
5ml/1 tsp fennel seeds
6 fresh thyme sprigs
2–3 bay leaves
good pinch of dried red
   chilli flakes
350g/12oz tomatoes, peeled, seeded
   and diced
5ml/1 tsp sun-dried tomato paste
good pinch of caster (superfine)
   sugar (optional)
75g/3oz/¾ cup black olives (optional)
salt and freshly ground black pepper

1 Cook the leeks in boiling salted water for 4–5 minutes. Use a large slotted spoon to remove the leeks and then place them in a strainer to drain thoroughly, cooling and reserving the cooking water in the pan. Squeeze out excess water and cut the leeks into 7.5cm/3in lengths.

2 Trim the fennel bulbs, reserving any feathery tops for the garnish and then cut the bulbs either into thin slices or into thicker wedges, according to taste.

--- NUTRITION NOTES ---

Per portion:

Energy	195kcals/806kJ
Protein	2.9g
Fat, total	17.2g
saturated fat	2.5g
Carbohydrate	6.2g
of which sugars	5.3g
Fibre	4.8g

3 Cook the fennel in the reserved cooking water for about 5 minutes, then drain thoroughly and toss with 30ml/2 tbsp of the olive oil. Season to taste with black pepper. Heat a ridged cast-iron griddle under the grill (broiler), then arrange the leeks and fennel on it. Cook until brown.

4 Remove the vegetables from the griddle, place in a large shallow dish and set aside.

5 Place the remaining olive oil, the shallots, white wine, 120ml/4fl oz/½ cup water, fennel seeds, thyme, bay leaves and chilli flakes in a large pan and bring to the boil over a medium heat. Lower the heat and simmer for about 10 minutes.

6 Add the diced tomatoes and cook briskly for 5–8 minutes, or until reduced and thickened.

7 Add the tomato paste and adjust the seasoning, adding a good pinch of caster sugar if you think the dressing needs it.

8 Pour the dressing over the leeks and fennel, toss to mix and leave to cool. If liked, the salad may be made several hours in advance and stored in the refrigerator, but bring it back to room temperature before serving.

9 To serve, stir the salad then scatter over the chopped fennel tops and black olives, if liked.

Grilled Onion and Aubergine Salad

Any longevity specialist will confirm that grilling is preferable to frying or boiling as a cooking method. Grilled aubergines are an unusual but tasty food, their flavour and health benefits much enhanced by the addition of sumac.

INGREDIENTS

Serves 6

3 aubergines (eggplant), cut into
  1cm/½in thick slices
675g/1½lb round, not flat, onions,
  thickly sliced
75–90ml/5–6 tbsp olive oil
5ml/1 tsp powdered sumac (optional)
45ml/3 tbsp roughly chopped flat
  leaf parsley
45ml/3 tbsp pine nuts, toasted
salt and freshly ground black pepper

For the dressing
2 garlic cloves
150ml/¼ pint/⅔ cup light tahini
juice of 1–2 lemons
45–60ml/3–4 tbsp water

1 Place the aubergine slices on a rack or in a strainer and sprinkle generously with salt. Leave them to sweat for 45–60 minutes, then rinse them thoroughly under cold running water and pat dry with kitchen paper.

2 Thread the sliced onions on to skewers or place them in an oiled wire grill (broiler) cage. Arrange the aubergine slices around the skewers on the grill cage.

3 Brush the aubergines and onions with about 45ml/3 tbsp of the oil and grill (broil) for 6–8 minutes on each side. Brush with more oil, if necessary, when you turn the vegetables. The vegetables should be browned and soft when cooked. The onions may need a little longer than the aubergines.

4 Arrange the vegetables on a serving dish and sprinkle with the sumac, if using, and season with salt and pepper to taste. Sprinkle with the remaining oil if they seem dry.

---- COOK'S TIP ----

• Sumac is a Mediterranean spice with a sharp, lemony taste. Buy it ready ground at Middle Eastern stores, good health food shops or delicatessens.
• Tahini is a thick, smooth, oily paste made from sesame seeds. It is also available from Middle Eastern stores, good health food shops and delicatessens and from some larger supermarkets.

5 For the dressing, crush the garlic in a mortar with a pinch of salt and gradually work in the tahini. Gradually work in the juice from one lemon, followed by the water. Taste and add more lemon juice if you think the dressing needs it. Thin with more water, if necessary, so that the dressing is fairly runny.

6 Drizzle the dressing over the salad and leave for 30–60 minutes, then sprinkle with the chopped parsley and pine nuts. Serve immediately at room temperature, not chilled.

---- NUTRITION NOTES ----

Per portion:

Energy	338kcals/1396kJ
Protein	7.7g
Fat, total	29.6g
saturated fat	3.8g
Carbohydrate	11.1g
of which sugars	8.2g
Fibre	5.2g

Red Rice Salad Niçoise

This salad is a real powerhouse of antioxidants and anti-ageing nutrients which is well worth the time involved. The fish provides high-quality protein and the red rice is preferable to ordinary white rice.

INGREDIENTS

Serves 4

about 675g/1½lb fresh tuna or
    swordfish, sliced into 2cm/¾in
    thick steaks
350g/12oz/1¾ cups Camargue red rice
fish or vegetable stock or water
450g/1lb French (green) beans
450g/1lb broad (fava) beans, shelled
1 cos (romaine) lettuce
450g/1lb cherry tomatoes, halved
    unless very tiny
30ml/2 tbsp coarsely chopped
    fresh coriander (cilantro)
3 hard-boiled (hard-cooked) eggs
175g/6oz/1½ cups pitted
    black olives
olive oil, for brushing

For the marinade

1 red onion, roughly chopped
2 garlic cloves
½ bunch fresh parsley
½ bunch fresh coriander (cilantro)
10ml/2 tsp paprika
45ml/3 tbsp olive oil
45ml/3 tbsp water
30ml/2 tbsp white wine vinegar
15ml/1 tbsp fresh lime or lemon juice
salt and freshly ground black pepper

For the dressing

30ml/2 tbsp fresh lime or lemon juice
5ml/1 tsp Dijon mustard
½ garlic clove, crushed (optional)
60ml/4 tbsp olive oil
60ml/4 tbsp sunflower oil

1 Make the marinade by mixing all the ingredients in a food processor and processing them for 30–40 seconds until the vegetables and herbs are all finely chopped.

2 Prick the tuna or swordfish steaks all over with a fork, lay them side by side in a shallow dish and pour over the marinade, turning the fish to coat each piece. Cover with clear film and leave in a cool place for 2–4 hours.

3 Cook the rice in stock or water, following the instructions on the packet, then drain, tip into a bowl and set aside.

4 Make the dressing. Mix the citrus juice, mustard and garlic, if using, in a bowl. Whisk in the oils, then add salt and freshly ground black pepper to taste. Stir 60ml/4 tbsp of the dressing into the rice, then spoon the rice into the centre of a large serving dish.

5 Cook the French beans and broad beans in boiling salted water until tender. Drain, refresh under cold water and drain again. Remove the outer shell from the broad beans and add all the beans to the rice.

6 Discard the outer leaves from the lettuce and tear the inner leaves into pieces. Add to the salad with the tomatoes and coriander. Shell the hard-boiled eggs and cut them into sixths. Preheat the grill (broiler).

7 Arrange the tuna or swordfish steaks on a grill pan. Brush with the marinade and a little extra olive oil. Grill (broil) for 3–4 minutes on each side, until the fish is tender and flakes easily when tested with the tip of a sharp knife. Brush with marinade and more olive oil when turning the fish.

8 Allow the fish to cool a little, then break the steaks into large pieces. Toss into the salad with the olives and the remaining dressing. Decorate with hard-boiled eggs and serve.

——— NUTRITION NOTES ———	
Per portion:	
Energy	600kcals/2527kJ
Protein	41.9g
Fat, total	22.2g
saturated fat	4g
Carbohydrate	62.1g
of which sugars	6.8g
Fibre	9.6g

Bean Salad with Tuna and Red Onion

INGREDIENTS

Serves 4
250g/9oz/1⅓ cups dried haricot
    (navy) or cannellini beans,
    soaked overnight
1 bay leaf
200–250g/7–9oz fine French
    (green) beans
1 large red onion, very thinly sliced
45ml/3 tbsp chopped fresh flat
    leaf parsley
200–250g/7–9oz good-quality canned
    tuna in olive oil, drained
200g/7oz cherry tomatoes, halved
salt and freshly ground black pepper
a few onion rings, to garnish

For the dressing
90ml/6 tbsp extra virgin olive oil
15ml/1 tbsp tarragon vinegar
5ml/1 tsp tarragon mustard
1 garlic clove, finely chopped
5ml/1 tsp grated lemon rind
a little lemon juice

1 Drain the beans and bring them to the boil in fresh water with the bay leaf added. Boil rapidly for 10 minutes, then reduce the heat and boil steadily for 1–1½ hours, until tender. The cooking time needed depends on the age of the beans. Drain them well. Discard the bay leaf.

2 Meanwhile, place all the dressing ingredients, apart from the lemon juice, in a jug (pitcher) and whisk until mixed. Season to taste with salt, pepper and lemon juice. Leave to stand.

3 Trim the French beans, then blanch them in boiling water for 3–4 minutes. Drain, refresh under cold water and drain thoroughly again.

4 Place both types of beans in a bowl. Add half the dressing and toss to mix. Stir in the onion and half the chopped parsley, then season to taste with salt and pepper.

5 Flake the tuna into large chunks with a knife and toss it into the beans with the tomato halves.

6 Arrange the salad on four individual plates. Drizzle the remaining dressing over the salad and scatter the remaining chopped parsley on top. Garnish with a few onion rings and serve at room temperature.

HEALTH BENEFITS

Oily fish, such as tuna, is an excellent source of essential fatty acids that help to keep the body protein and DNA in good condition.

NUTRITION NOTES

Per portion:

Energy	395kcals/1660kJ
Protein	27.2g
Fat, total	18.1g
saturated fat	2.6g
Carbohydrate	33.1g
of which sugars	5.9g
Fibre	11.8g

Baked Sweet Potato Salad

Sweet potatoes are not only very tasty but also full of energy. This dish is best appreciated if served with other tropical dishes.

INGREDIENTS

Serves 4
1kg/2¼lb sweet potatoes

For the dressing
45ml/3 tbsp chopped fresh
   coriander (cilantro)
juice of 1 lime
150ml/¼ pint/⅔ cup natural yogurt

For the salad
1 red (bell) pepper, seeded and
   finely diced
3 celery sticks, finely diced
¼ red onion, finely chopped
1 red chilli, finely chopped
salt and freshly ground black pepper
coriander (cilantro) leaves, to garnish

1 Preheat the oven to 200°C/400°F/ Gas 6. Wash and pierce the potatoes all over and bake them in the oven for 40 minutes or until tender.

— NUTRITION NOTES —

Per portion:

Energy	172kcals/732kJ
Protein	3.7g
Fat, total	0.8g
saturated fat	0.3g
Carbohydrate	39.9g
of which sugars	13.6g
Fibre	4.7g

2 Meanwhile, mix the three dressing ingredients together in a bowl and season to taste. Chill while you prepare the remaining ingredients.

3 In a large bowl mix the red pepper, celery, onion and chilli together.

4 Remove the potatoes from the oven and when cool enough to handle, peel them. Cut the potatoes into cubes and add them to the bowl. Drizzle the dressing over and toss carefully. Season again to taste and serve, garnished with fresh coriander.

MAIN MEALS

Fresh vegetables, oily fish and lean meat all play an essential part

in anti-ageing nutrition. This chapter is filled with recipes that

will help to keep you feeling younger and healthier for longer.

Vegetable Stew with Roasted Tomato Sauce is a great source of the

age-defying nutrients betacarotene and lycopene, while Lentil Dhal

will invigorate the body and Salmon and Black-eyed Bean Stew

will help keep your cells in good shape.

Leek Terrine with Red Peppers

Red peppers are an excellent source of age-defying phytochemicals – plant nutrients necessary for optimal health.

INGREDIENTS

Serves 6-8
1.8kg/4lb slender leeks
4 large red (bell) peppers, halved
 and seeded
15ml/1 tbsp extra virgin olive oil
10ml/2 tsp balsamic vinegar
5ml/1 tsp ground roasted cumin seeds
salt and freshly ground black pepper

For the dressing
120ml/4fl oz/½ cup extra virgin olive oil
1 garlic clove, bruised and peeled
5ml/1 tsp Dijon mustard
5ml/1 tsp soy sauce
15ml/1 tbsp balsamic vinegar
2.5–5ml/½–1 tsp ground roasted
 cumin seeds
15–30ml/1–2 tbsp chopped mixed
 fresh basil and flat leaf parsley

1 Line a 23cm/9in-long terrine or loaf tin (pan) with clear film (plastic wrap), leaving the ends overhanging. Cut the leeks to the length of the tin.

2 Cook the leeks in boiling salted water for 5–7 minutes, until just tender. Drain thoroughly and allow to cool, then squeeze out as much water as possible from the leeks and leave them to drain on a clean dish towel.

3 Grill (broil) the red peppers, skin side uppermost, until the skin blisters and blackens. Place them in a bowl, cover and leave for 10 minutes. Peel the peppers and cut the flesh into long strips, then place them in a bowl and add the oil, vinegar and cumin seeds. Season to taste and toss well.

4 Layer the leeks and strips of red pepper in the lined tin, alternating the layers so that the white of the leeks in one row is covered by the green of the next row. Season the leeks.

5 Cover with the overhanging clear film. Top with a plate and weigh it down with food cans or scale weights. Chill for several hours or overnight.

6 To make the dressing, place the oil, garlic, mustard, soy sauce and vinegar in a jug (pitcher) and mix thoroughly. Season, then add ground cumin to taste and leave to stand for several hours. Discard the garlic and add the fresh herbs to the dressing.

7 Unmould the leek terrine and cut it into thick slices. Put one or two slices on each plate, drizzle with the dressing and serve.

NUTRITION NOTES	
Per portion:	
Energy	187kcals/776kJ
Protein	4.4g
Fat, total	14g
saturated fat	2.1g
Carbohydrate	11.3g
of which sugars	9.5g
Fibre	6.2g

Stuffed Peppers

Throughout the Middle East and Mediterranean, couscous is lauded for its health-giving properties.

INGREDIENTS

Serves 4
6 (bell) peppers
30ml/2 tbsp sunflower oil
1 onion, finely chopped
5ml/1 tsp olive oil
2.5ml/½ tsp salt
175g/6oz/1 cup couscous
25g/1oz/2 tbsp raisins
30ml/2 tbsp chopped fresh mint
1 egg yolk
salt and freshly ground black pepper
fresh mint leaves, to garnish

1 Preheat the oven to 200°C/400°F/ Gas 6. Slit each pepper and remove the core and seeds. Heat the oil in a pan, add the onion and cook until soft.

2 To cook the couscous, bring 250ml/8fl oz/1 cup water to the boil. Add the oil and the salt, then remove the pan from the heat and add the couscous. Stir and leave to stand, covered, for 5 minutes.

3 Stir the cooked onion, raisins and mint into the couscous, then season well with salt and freshly ground black pepper. Stir in the egg yolk.

— NUTRITION NOTES —	
Per portion:	
Energy	327kcals/1376kJ
Protein	6.5g
Fat, total	9.4g
saturated fat	1.8g
Carbohydrate	57g
of which sugars	18.9g
Fibre	4.1g

4 Using a teaspoon, fill the peppers with the couscous mixture to only about three-quarters full, because the couscous will increase in size when it is cooked further.

5 Place the peppers in a lightly oiled ovenproof dish and bake, uncovered, for about 20 minutes until tender. Serve hot or cold, garnished with the mint leaves.

Barley Risotto with Roasted Squash

Pumpkin seeds, walnuts and garlic are excellent anti-agers.

INGREDIENTS

Serves 4–5

200g/7oz/1 cup pearl barley

1 butternut squash, peeled, seeded and cut into chunks

10ml/2 tsp chopped fresh thyme

60ml/4 tbsp olive oil

4 leeks, cut into fairly thick diagonal slices

2 garlic cloves, finely chopped

175g/6oz chestnut mushrooms, sliced

2 carrots, coarsely grated

about 120ml/4fl oz/½ cup good-quality vegetable stock

30ml/2 tbsp chopped fresh flat leaf parsley

50g/2oz Pecorino cheese, grated or shaved

45ml/3 tbsp pumpkin seeds, toasted, or chopped walnuts

salt and freshly ground black pepper

1 Place the barley in a strainer and rinse thoroughly, then cook it in simmering water, keeping the pan part-covered, for 35–45 minutes, or until tender. Drain well. Preheat the oven to 200°C/400°F/Gas 6.

2 Place the squash in a roasting tin (pan) with half the chopped fresh thyme. Season with pepper and toss with half the oil. Roast, stirring once, for 30–35 minutes, until tender and beginning to brown.

3 Heat the remaining oil in a frying pan. Cook the leeks and garlic for 5 minutes.

4 Add the mushrooms and remaining chopped thyme to the pan, then cook until the liquid from the mushrooms evaporates and they begin to fry.

5 Stir in the grated carrots and cook for about 2 minutes, then add the pearl barley and most of the stock. Season well and part-cover the pan. Cook for a further 5 minutes. Pour in the remaining stock if the mixture seems dry.

6 Add the parsley and half the Pecorino cheese to the vegetables, then stir in the roasted squash. Season with salt and black pepper to taste and serve immediately, sprinkled with the toasted pumpkin seeds or chopped walnuts and the remaining Pecorino.

NUTRITION NOTES	
Per portion:	
Energy	419kcals/1768kJ
Protein	10.2g
Fat, total	14.5g
saturated fat	3.9g
Carbohydrate	66.3g
of which sugars	11g
Fibre	5.7g

Vegetable Stew with Roasted Tomato Sauce

INGREDIENTS

Serves 6

45ml/3 tbsp olive oil
250g/9oz small pickling (pearl) onions or shallots
1 large onion, chopped
2 garlic cloves, chopped
5ml/1 tsp cumin seeds
5ml/1 tsp ground coriander seeds
5ml/1 tsp paprika
10cm/4in piece cinnamon stick
2 fresh bay leaves
300–450ml/½–¾ pint/1¼–scant 2 cups good vegetable stock
good pinch of saffron strands
450g/1lb carrots, thickly sliced
2 green (bell) peppers, seeded and thickly sliced
115g/4oz ready-to-eat dried apricots, halved if large
5–7.5ml/1–1½ tsp ground toasted cumin seeds
450g/1lb squash, peeled, seeded and cut into chunks
pinch of sugar, to taste
salt and ground black pepper
45ml/3 tbsp fresh coriander (cilantro) leaves, to garnish

For the roasted tomato and garlic sauce

1kg/2¼lb tomatoes, halved
45ml/3 tbsp olive oil
1–2 fresh red chillies, seeded and chopped
2–3 garlic cloves, chopped
5ml/1 tsp fresh thyme leaves

1 Preheat the oven to 180°C/350°F/ Gas 4. First make the sauce. Place the tomatoes, cut sides uppermost, in a roasting tin (pan). Season well, drizzle with the olive oil and roast for 30 minutes.

2 Scatter the chillies, garlic and thyme over the tomatoes, stir to mix and roast for a further 30–45 minutes, until the tomatoes are collapsed but still juicy. Cool, then process in a food processor or blender to make a thick sauce. Strain to remove the seeds.

3 Heat 30ml/2 tbsp of the oil in a large pan and cook the pickling onions or shallots until browned.

4 Remove the onions from the pan and set aside. Add the remaining oil and chopped onion and cook for 5–7 minutes. Stir in the garlic and cumin and cook for 3–4 minutes.

5 Add the ground coriander seeds, paprika, cinnamon stick and bay leaves to the pan. Cook, stirring constantly, for 2 minutes, then mix in the vegetable stock, saffron, carrots and green peppers. Season well, cover and simmer gently for 10 minutes. Stir in the apricots, 5ml/1 tsp of the ground cumin, the onions or shallots, the squash and the tomato sauce.

6 Cover the pan and cook for a further 5 minutes. Uncover and continue to cook, stirring occasionally, for 10–15 minutes, until the vegetables are all fully cooked.

7 Adjust the seasoning, adding a little more cumin and a pinch of sugar to taste. Remove and discard the cinnamon stick. Serve scattered with the fresh coriander leaves.

Indian Rice with Tomatoes and Spinach

Although white rice accelerates the ageing process, brown rice is actually an ideal anti-ageing food.

INGREDIENTS

Serves 4

45ml/3 tbsp sunflower oil
1 onion, chopped
2 garlic cloves, crushed
3 tomatoes, peeled, seeded and chopped
225g/8oz/generous 1 cup brown basmati rice, soaked
5ml/1 tsp ground coriander
5ml/1 tsp ground cumin
2 carrots, coarsely grated
900ml/1½ pints/3¾ cups good-quality vegetable stock
275g/10oz baby spinach leaves, washed
50g/2oz/½ cup unsalted cashew nuts, toasted
salt and freshly ground black pepper

1 Heat the oil in a flameproof casserole and fry the onion and garlic for 4–5 minutes until soft. Add the chopped tomatoes to the pan and cook for 3–4 minutes, stirring, until slightly thickened.

2 Drain the rice, then add it to the casserole and allow to cook gently for 1–2 minutes, stirring, until the rice is well coated with the tomato and onion mixture.

3 Stir the coriander and cumin into the mixture, then add the carrots and season with salt and ground black pepper. Pour in the stock and stir well to combine.

4 Bring the mixture to the boil, then cover tightly with a lid and simmer over a very gentle heat for about 25 minutes until the rice is tender.

5 Lay the spinach on the surface of the rice, cover again and cook for 2–3 minutes until the spinach has wilted. Fold the wilted leaves into the rice and check the seasoning. Sprinkle with the toasted cashew nuts and serve.

NUTRITION NOTES	
Per portion:	
Energy	328kcals/1382kJ
Protein	9g
Fat, total	9.5g
saturated fat	1.9g
Carbohydrate	54.8g
of which sugars	7.6g
Fibre	4.5g

Lentil Dhal

Ayurvedic (ancient Indian) practitioners use several of the ingredients of this dish. Ideally served with brown rice, it makes a delicious and invigorating meal.

INGREDIENTS

Serves 4-6
45ml/3 tbsp olive oil
1 onion, chopped
2 green chillies, seeded and chopped
15ml/1 tbsp chopped fresh
   root ginger
225g/8oz/1 cup yellow or red lentils
900ml/1½ pints/3¾ cups water
45ml/3 tbsp roasted garlic purée (paste)
5ml/1 tsp ground cumin
5ml/1 tsp ground coriander
200g/7oz tomatoes, peeled and diced
a little lemon juice
salt and freshly ground black pepper
30–45ml/2–3 tbsp coriander (cilantro)
   sprigs and fried onion and garlic
   slices, to garnish

For the whole spice mix
30ml/2 tbsp sunflower oil
4–5 shallots, sliced
2 garlic cloves, thinly sliced
5ml/1 tsp cumin seeds
5ml/1 tsp mustard seeds
3–4 small dried red chillies
8–10 fresh curry leaves

1 Heat the olive oil in a large pan, add the chopped onion, chillies and ginger and cook for 10 minutes, until golden.

2 Stir in the lentils and water, bring to the boil, then reduce the heat and part-cover the pan with a lid. Simmer, stirring occasionally, for about 55 minutes, until it has a similar texture to very thick soup.

3 Stir in the roasted garlic purée, cumin and ground coriander, then season with salt and pepper to taste. Cook for a further 10–15 minutes, uncovered, stirring frequently.

4 Stir in the tomatoes and then adjust the seasoning, adding a little lemon juice to taste.

5 To make the whole spice mix, heat the oil in a small, heavy-based pan. Add the shallots and fry over a medium heat, stirring occasionally, until crisp and browned. Add the garlic and cook, stirring, until it colours slightly. Use a slotted spoon to remove the mixture from the pan and set aside.

6 Add the cumin and mustard seeds to the remaining oil and fry until the mustard seeds pop. Stir in the chillies, curry leaves and shallot mixture, then immediately swirl into the dhal. Garnish with coriander sprigs, onions and garlic and serve.

Salmon and Black-eyed Bean Stew

Oily fish, such as salmon, are good for lowering cholesterol and easing the symptoms of arthritis. They may also help to reduce the risk of cancer.

INGREDIENTS

Serves 2 as a main meal

150g/5oz salmon fillet, boned and skinned
400g/14oz canned black-eyed beans (peas) in brine
50g/2oz fresh shiitake mushrooms, stalks removed
50g/2oz carrot, peeled
50g/2oz mooli (daikon), peeled
5g/⅛oz dashi-konbu (dried kelp seaweed) about 10cm/4in square
60ml/4 tbsp water
15ml/1 tbsp shoyu (ordinary soy sauce)
7.5ml/1½ tsp mirin
salt
2.5cm/1in fresh root ginger, peeled, to garnish

1 Slice the salmon into 1cm/½in-thick pieces. Thoroughly salt the fillet and leave for 1 hour.

2 Wash away the salt and cut into 1cm/½in small cubes. Par-boil in rapidly boiling water in a small pan for 30 seconds and drain. Gently wash under running water.

3 Slice the ginger for the garnish thinly lengthways, then stack the slices and cut them into thin threads. Soak in cold water for about 30 minutes, then drain well.

4 Drain the can of black-eyed beans and keep the liquid in a medium pan. Set both aside.

5 Chop all the vegetables into 1cm/½in cubes. Wipe the dashi-konbu (dried kelp seaweed) with a damp dish towel or kitchen paper, then snip with scissors. Cut everything as close to the same size as possible.

6 Put the par-boiled salmon, dashi-konbu and vegetables into the pan containing the liquid from the beans (peas) can. Pour the beans on top and add the water and 1.5ml/¼ tsp salt. Bring to the boil. Reduce the heat to low and cook for 6 minutes or until the carrot is cooked.

7 Add the shoyu and cook for a further 4 minutes. Add the mirin and remove the pan from the heat. Mix well and check the seasoning. Leave to rest for an hour.

8 Serve the stew warm or cold in a medium bowl or in individual small bowls. Garnish with the threads of ginger on top.

HEALTH BENEFITS

Salmon is an excellent source of health-promoting essential fatty acids and valuable B vitamins, which can affect methylation – a process that keeps our DNA in good condition.

NUTRITION NOTES

Per portion:

Energy	190kcals/803kJ
Protein	16g
Fat, total	5.3g
saturated fat	1.1g
Carbohydrate	20.9g
of which sugars	2g
Fibre	3.9g

Baked Trout with Almonds and Lime

Nothing beats a fresh, baked trout with almonds. Trout is an oily fish, while almonds supply extra vitamin E for efficient antioxidant protection.

INGREDIENTS

Serves 4
2 fresh pasilla chillies
4 rainbow trout, cleaned
4 garlic cloves
10ml/2 tsp dried oregano
juice of 2 limes
50g/2oz/½ cup slivered almonds
salt and freshly ground black pepper

1 Roast the chillies in a dry frying pan or griddle until the skins are blistered, being careful not to let the flesh burn. Put them in a strong polythene bag and tie to keep the steam in. Set aside for 20 minutes.

2 Meanwhile, rub a little salt into the cavities in the trout, to ensure that they are completely clean, then rinse them under cold running water. Drain and pat dry with kitchen paper.

3 Remove the roast chillies from the plastic bag and peel off the skins. Cut off the stems, then slit the chillies and scrape out the seeds. Chop the flesh roughly and put it in a mortar. Crush with a pestle until the mixture forms a paste.

4 Place the chilli paste in a shallow dish that will hold all the trout in a single layer. Slice the garlic lengthwise and add to the dish.

5 Add the oregano and 10ml/2 tsp salt, then stir in the lime juice and pepper to taste. Add the trout, turning to coat them in the mixture. Cover the dish and then set them aside for at least 30 minutes, turning the trout again halfway through.

6 Preheat the oven to 200°C/400°F/ Gas 6. Have ready four pieces of foil, each one large enough to wrap a trout. Top each sheet with greaseproof (waxed) paper of the same size.

7 Place one of the trout on one of the pieces of paper, moisten with the marinade, then sprinkle about a quarter of the almonds on top. Bring up the sides of the paper and fold over to seal in the fish, then fold the foil over to make a neat parcel. Make three more parcels in the same way, then place them side by side in a large roasting tin (pan).

8 Transfer the parcels to the oven and bake for 25 minutes. Put each parcel on a serving plate, or open them in the kitchen and serve unwrapped.

NUTRITION NOTES	
Per portion:	
Energy	243kcals/1021kJ
Protein	37g
Fat, total	10.4g
saturated fat	1.9g
Carbohydrate	0.4g
of which sugars	0.3g
Fibre	0.5g

Salmon en Papillote

INGREDIENTS

25ml/1½ tbsp sunflower oil
2 yellow (bell) peppers, seeded and
 thinly sliced
4cm/1½in fresh root ginger, peeled
 and finely shredded
1 large fennel bulb, finely sliced,
 feathery tops chopped and reserved
1 fresh green chilli, seeded and
 finely shredded
2 large leeks, cut into 10cm/4in lengths
 and shredded lengthways
30ml/2 tbsp snipped chives
10ml/2 tsp light soy sauce
6 portions salmon fillet, each weighing
 150–175g/5–6oz, skinned
10ml/2 tsp toasted sesame oil
salt and freshly ground black pepper

1 Heat the oil in a large non-stick frying pan and cook the yellow peppers, ginger and fennel for about 5 minutes, until they are softened but have not browned. Add the chilli and shredded leeks and cook for a further 2–3 minutes. Stir in half the chives and the soy sauce with seasoning to taste. Set aside to cool.

2 Preheat the oven to 190°C/375°F/ Gas 5. Cut six 35cm/14in circles of baking parchment or foil.

3 Divide the vegetable mixture among the six circles and place a portion of salmon on each pile of vegetables. Drizzle with toasted sesame oil and sprinkle with the remaining snipped chives and the chopped fennel tops. Season with salt and pepper.

HEALTH BENEFITS

Salmon is rich in essential fatty acids and yellow peppers are rich in the antioxidant nutrient, betacarotene.

4 Fold the paper or foil over to enclose the fish, rolling and twisting the edges together to seal the parcels. Place the parcels on a baking sheet and bake for 15–20 minutes, until the parcels are puffed up and, if made with paper, lightly browned.

5 Transfer the parcels to warmed individual plates and serve.

NUTRITION NOTES

Per portion:
Energy	333kcals/1386kJ
Protein	29.1g
Fat, total	22g
saturated fat	3.8g
Carbohydrate	5g
of which sugars	4.6g
Fibre	2.7g

Moroccan Spiced Mackerel

This combination of mackerel and spices is packed with vital omega-3 fatty acids, the "good" fats which are so essential to our health and well-being.

INGREDIENTS

Serves 4

150ml/¼ pint/⅔ cup sunflower oil
15ml/1 tbsp paprika
5–10ml/1–2 tsp harissa or chilli powder
10ml/2 tsp ground cumin
10ml/2 tsp ground coriander
2 garlic cloves, crushed
juice of 2 lemons
30ml/2 tbsp chopped fresh mint leaves
30ml/2 tbsp chopped fresh
 coriander (cilantro)
4 mackerel, cleaned
salt and freshly ground black pepper
mint sprigs, to garnish
lemon wedges, to serve

1 In a bowl, whisk together the oil, spices, crushed garlic and lemon juice. Season, then stir in the chopped mint and coriander to make a spicy marinade for the fish.

2 Use a sharp knife to make two or three diagonal slashes on either side of each mackerel. Pour the marinade into a shallow non-metallic dish that is large enough to hold all of the fish in a single layer.

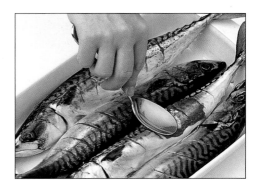

3 Put in the mackerel and turn them over in the marinade, spooning it into the slashes so that they absorb as much as possible.

4 Cover the dish and leave to marinate for 3 hours.

5 When you are ready to cook the mackerel, preheat the grill (broiler) to medium-high. Transfer the fish to a rack set over a grilling (broiling) pan and grill (broil) for 5–7 minutes on each side until just cooked, turning the fish once and basting them several times with the spicy marinade.

6 Serve the mackerel hot or cold with lemon wedges, garnished with mint sprigs. Herb-flavoured couscous or boiled brown rice make good anti-ageing accompaniments.

COOK'S TIP

These spicy mackerel can be cooked on a barbecue. Making sure the coals are very hot, arrange the fish on a large hinged rack to make turning easier and barbecue for 5–7 minutes, turning once.

NUTRITION NOTES

Per portion:

Energy	716kcals/2964kJ
Protein	41.8g
Fat, total	60.8g
saturated fat	10.2g
Carbohydrate	0.2g
of which sugars	0.2g
Fibre	0g

Smoked Haddock with Mustard Cabbage

This simple dish makes a good, nutritious meal and deserves to be high on your age-defying recipe list.

INGREDIENTS

Serves 4

1 Savoy or pointu cabbage
675g/1½lb undyed smoked haddock fillet
300ml/½ pint/1¼ cups milk
½ onion, peeled and sliced into rings
2 bay leaves
½ lemon, sliced
4 white peppercorns
4 ripe tomatoes
45ml/3 tbsp olive oil
30ml/2 tbsp wholegrain mustard
juice of 1 lemon
salt and freshly ground black pepper
30ml/2 tbsp chopped fresh parsley,
   to garnish

1 Cut the Savoy or pointu cabbage in half with a sharp knife. Remove the central core and thick ribs, then shred the cabbage.

2 Cook in a pan of lightly salted boiling water, or steam over boiling water for about 10 minutes, until just tender. Leave in the pan or steamer until required.

3 Meanwhile, put the haddock in a large shallow pan with the milk, onion and bay leaves. Add the lemon slices and peppercorns. Bring to simmering point, cover and poach for 8–10 minutes until the fish flakes easily when it is tested with the tip of a sharp knife. Take the pan off the heat and set aside. Preheat the grill (broiler).

4 Halve the tomatoes horizontally, season them with salt and pepper and grill (broil) until lightly browned. Drain the cabbage, refresh it under cold water and drain again.

5 Heat the oil in a shallow pan or wok, add the cabbage and toss over the heat for 2 minutes. Mix in the mustard and season to taste, then tip the cabbage into a warmed serving dish.

6 Drain the haddock. Skin and cut the fish into four pieces. Place on top of the cabbage with some onion and tomato. Pour on the lemon juice, sprinkle with parsley and serve.

NUTRITION NOTES	
Per portion:	
Energy	282kcals/1184kJ
Protein	33.2g
Fat, total	10.9g
saturated fat	2.1g
Carbohydrate	13.3g
of which sugars	12.8g
Fibre	3.5g

Chinese-style Steamed Fish

This dish is mouth-watering as well as rejuvenating, and provides useful nutrients to help repair age-related damage. Make it even more nutritious by serving it with stir-fried vegetables such as mushrooms and carrots, as well as with other dark-coloured vegetables.

INGREDIENTS

Serves 4–6

2 sea bass, grey mullet or trout, each
   weighing about 675–800g/1½–1¾lb
25ml/1½ tbsp salted black beans
30ml/2 tbsp finely shredded fresh
   root ginger
4 garlic cloves, thinly sliced
30ml/2 tbsp Chinese rice wine or
   dry sherry
30ml/2 tbsp light soy sauce
4–6 spring onions (scallions), finely
   shredded or sliced diagonally
45ml/3 tbsp sunflower oil
10ml/2 tsp sesame oil

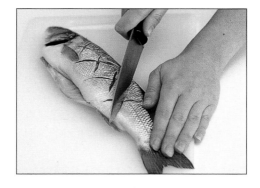

1 Wash the fish inside and out under cold running water, then pat them dry on kitchen paper. Using a sharp knife, slash three or four deep cross shapes on each side of each fish.

2 Mash half the black beans in a small bowl and then stir in the remaining whole beans.

3 Place a little ginger and garlic inside the cavity of each fish and then lay them on a plate or dish.

4 Rub the bean mixture into the fish, especially into the slashes, then scatter the remaining ginger and garlic over the top. Cover and chill for 30 minutes.

5 Place the plate inside a steamer over a pan of boiling water. Sprinkle the rice wine or sherry and half the soy sauce over and steam for 15–20 minutes, or until just cooked.

6 Sprinkle the cooked fish with the remaining soy sauce and then scatter the shredded or sliced spring onions over the top.

7 In a small pan, heat the sunflower oil until it is smoking, then drizzle it over the spring onions on top of the fish. Finally, sprinkle with the sesame oil and then serve the fish immediately.

— NUTRITION NOTES —	
Per portion:	
Energy	240kcals/1010kJ
Protein	41.5g
Fat, total	8.1g
saturated fat	1.9g
Carbohydrate	0.3g
of which sugars	0.3g
Fibre	0.1g

Romanian Chicken Stew

INGREDIENTS

Serves 6

60ml/4 tbsp sunflower oil
1 mild onion, thinly sliced
2 garlic cloves, crushed
2 red peppers (bell), seeded
    and sliced
about 1.5kg/3½lb chicken
90ml/6 tbsp tomato purée (paste)
3 potatoes, diced
5ml/1 tsp chopped fresh rosemary
5ml/1 tsp chopped fresh marjoram
5ml/1 tsp chopped fresh thyme
3 carrots, cut into chunks
½ small celeriac, cut into chunks
120ml/4fl oz/½ cup chicken stock
2 courgettes (zucchini), sliced
salt and freshly ground black pepper
chopped fresh rosemary and
    marjoram, to garnish
dark rye bread, to serve

1 Heat the oil in a large flameproof casserole. Add the onion and garlic and cook for 1–2 minutes until soft; then add the red peppers.

2 Joint the chicken into six pieces, place in the casserole and brown gently on all sides.

─── HEALTH BENEFITS ───

Lean chicken contains carnosine, which is present in brain, muscle and eye tissue.

3 After about 15 minutes add the tomato purée, potatoes, herbs, carrots, celeriac and chicken stock, and season to taste with salt and pepper. Cook over a gentle heat, covered, for a further 40–50 minutes.

4 Add the courgette slices 5 minutes before the end of cooking. Adjust the seasoning to taste. Garnish with the fresh rosemary and marjoram and serve with dark rye bread.

─── NUTRITION NOTES ───

Per portion:

Energy	466kcals/1937kJ
Protein	25.8g
Fat, total	30.2g
saturated fat	8.4g
Carbohydrate	23.9g
of which sugars	11.5g
Fibre	3.7g

Chicken with Forty Cloves of Garlic

The benefits of garlic have been known since antiquity. Use it liberally and frequently.

INGREDIENTS

Serves 6
5–6 whole heads of garlic
45ml/3 tbsp olive oil
1.8–2kg/4–4½lb chicken
150g/5oz/1¼ cups plain (all-purpose) flour, plus 5ml/1 tsp
75ml/5 tbsp white port or other white, fortified wine
2–3 fresh tarragon or rosemary sprigs
few drops of lemon juice (optional)
salt and freshly ground black pepper

1 Separate three of the heads of garlic into individual cloves and peel them. Remove the first layer of papery skin from the remaining heads of garlic and cut off the tops to expose the cloves, if you like, or alternatively leave them whole. Preheat the oven to 180°C/350°F/Gas 4.

2 Heat the olive oil in a flameproof casserole or ovenproof pan that is just large enough to take the chicken and the garlic. Add the chicken and cook over a medium heat, turning frequently, for 10–15 minutes, until it is browned on all sides.

3 Sprinkle 5ml/1 tsp flour into the casserole or pan and cook for a further 1 minute. Add the port or fortified wine. Tuck in the heads of garlic and the peeled cloves with the herb sprigs. Pour over the remaining oil and season.

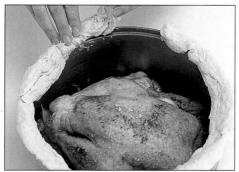

4 Mix the main batch of flour with water to make a firm dough. Roll into a long sausage and press it around the rim of the casserole, then press on the lid, folding the dough over to create a seal. Roast the chicken and garlic for 1½ hours.

5 To serve, lift off the lid to break the seal and remove the chicken and whole garlic to a serving platter and keep warm.

6 Remove and discard the herb sprigs, then place the casserole on the hob and whisk to combine the peeled garlic cloves with the juices. Add a little lemon juice to taste. Pour the sauce into a food processor or blender and process until smooth. Alternatively, press through a strainer for a smoother result. Serve the sauce with the chicken.

NUTRITION NOTES	
Per portion:	
Energy	468kcals/1946kJ
Protein	32.5g
Fat, total	32g
saturated fat	10.6g
Carbohydrate	8.8g
of which sugars	1.9g
Fibre	0.3g

Skewered Lamb with Coriander Yogurt

INGREDIENTS

Serves 4
900g/2lb lean boneless lamb
1 large onion, grated
3 bay leaves
5 thyme or rosemary sprigs
grated rind and juice of 1 lemon
2.5ml/½ tsp caster (superfine) sugar
75ml/2½fl oz/⅓ cup olive oil
salt and freshly ground black pepper
sprigs of rosemary, to garnish
grilled (broiled) lemon wedges,
    to serve

For the coriander yogurt
150ml/¼ pint/⅔ cup thick
    natural (plain) yogurt
15ml/1 tbsp chopped fresh mint
15ml/1 tbsp chopped fresh
    coriander (cilantro)
10ml/2 tsp grated onion

1 To make the coriander yogurt, mix together the yogurt, mint, coriander and grated onion and transfer to a serving dish and chill.

2 To make the kebabs, cut the lamb into small chunks and put in a bowl. Mix together the grated onion, bay leaves, thyme or rosemary sprigs, lemon rind and juice, sugar and oil, then season and pour over the lamb.

3 Mix the ingredients together. Leave to marinate in the refrigerator for several hours or overnight.

4 Remove the lamb chunks from the marinade and thread on to skewers.

5 Arrange the skewers on a grill (broiler) rack and cook under a preheated grill (broiler) for about 10 minutes until browned, turning occasionally. Transfer the skewers to a plate and garnish with rosemary sprigs. Serve with the grilled lemon wedges and the coriander yogurt.

HEALTH BENEFITS

Lean red meat, such as lamb, contains a host of anti-ageing substances, including carnosine, vitamin K and conjugated linoleic acid. Vitamin K is believed to reduce the risk of osteoporosis and heart disease in later life and conjugated linoleic acid is believed to help lower cholesterol levels in the body. The coriander yogurt offers useful amounts of calcium, which is needed for healthy bones.

NUTRITION NOTES

Per portion:

Energy	511kcals/2135kJ
Protein	49.2g
Fat, total	32.7g
saturated fat	11.4g
Carbohydrate	5.8g
of which sugars	4.9g
Fibre	0.5g

Pan-fried Calf's Liver

Liver provides vitamin E and should be consumed at least once or twice a month. The delicious aroma of cooked liver is truly mouth-watering. Frying, although in general best avoided, is fine if done infrequently.

INGREDIENTS

45ml/3 tbsp olive oil
4 onions, finely sliced
4 slices calf's liver, each weighing
  about 115g/4oz
30ml/2 tbsp plain (all-purpose) flour
30ml/2 tbsp olive oil
salt and freshly ground black pepper
chopped fresh parsley, to garnish

1 Heat the olive oil in a large, heavy pan with a tight-fitting lid. Add the onions and mix well to coat with oil. Cover the pan and cook gently for 10 minutes, stirring occasionally.

2 Cook the onions for a further 10 minutes, until soft. Increase the heat, remove the lid and stir the onions over a high heat until they are deep golden and crisp. Use a slotted spoon to remove the onions from the pan, draining off as much oil as possible.

3 Meanwhile, rinse the calf's liver in cold water and pat it dry on kitchen paper. Season the flour with salt and pepper, put it on a plate and turn the slices of liver in it until they are lightly coated in flour.

NUTRITION NOTES	
Per portion:	
Energy	327kcals/1399kJ
Protein	24g
Fat, total	22.3g
saturated fat	4.5g
Carbohydrate	8.1g
of which sugars	4.2g
Fibre	1g

4 Heat the olive oil in a large, heavy frying pan, add the floured slices of liver and cook for about 2 minutes on each side, or until they are lightly browned and just firm.

5 Remove the pan from the heat and arrange the pan-fried liver on warmed plates, with the crisp, golden onions. Garnish with chopped parsley and serve with potatoes and plenty of leafy green vegetables.

DESSERTS AND BAKES

Although sugar is thought to be one of the worst culprits among the foods that can accelerate ageing, you don't have to miss out on desserts, cakes and cookies entirely. This chapter is devoted to tasty sweet treats that are low in sugar and packed with anti-ageing ingredients. Try a scoop of hormone-balancing Date and Tofu Ice, a bowl of free radical blitzing Poached Winter Fruits or lutein-rich Blueberry and Orange Crêpe Baskets.

Peach and Cardamom Yogurt Ice

After a satisfying main course, what better way to finish off your feast than with a light dessert. Using natural yogurt instead of cream is a real bonus, as it keeps the calorie content down.

INGREDIENTS

Serves 6

8 cardamom pods
6 peaches, total weight about 500g/
    1¼lb, peeled, halved and
    stoned (pitted)
30ml/2 tbsp water
200ml/7fl oz/scant 1 cup live
    natural (plain) yogurt

1 Put the cardamom pods on a board and crush them with the bottom of a ramekin, or place them in a mortar and crush them with a pestle.

2 Chop the peaches roughly and put them in a pan. Add the crushed cardamom pods, together with their black seeds and the water. Cover the pan and allow to simmer for about 10 minutes or until the fruit is tender. Leave to cool.

3 Tip the peach mixture into a food processor or blender, process until the mixture is smooth, then use a wooden spoon to press through a strainer placed over a large bowl.

4 **By hand:** Add the yogurt to the peach and cardomom purée and mix together in the bowl. Pour into a plastic tub and freeze for about 5 hours until firm, beating once or twice with a fork or an electric whisk to break up the ice crystals.

Using an ice cream maker: Churn the peach and cardamom purée until thick, then scrape it into a plastic tub or similar container. Stir in the natural yogurt and freeze until firm enough to hold a scoop shape.

5 Use an ice cream scoop to make balls of ice cream. Arrange on a large platter, and serve immediately.

HEALTH BENEFITS

Fresh peaches are full of essential vitamins and minerals, such as antioxidant vitamin C and betacarotene, which help to neutralize free radicals that can damage the body. Live natural yogurt is full of healthy bacteria that can aid effective digestion.

NUTRITION NOTES

Per portion:	
Energy	69kcals/296kJ
Protein	3.8g
Fat, total	0.5g
saturated fat	0.3g
Carbohydrate	13.3g
of which sugars	13.3g
Fibre	1.9g

Date and Tofu Ice

This unusual combination of ingredients provides a substantial amount of soya, which not only helps to alleviate the symptoms of the menopause, but is also beneficial for younger people, both male and female, as it helps to maintain optimal hormone balance.

INGREDIENTS

Serves 6

250g/9oz/1½ cups stoned (pitted) dates
600ml/1 pint/2½ cups apple juice
5ml/1 tsp ground cinnamon
285g/10½oz pack chilled beancurd
  (tofu), drained and cubed
150ml/¼ pint/⅔ cup unsweetened
  soya milk

1 Put the dates in a pan. Pour in 300ml/½ pint/1¼ cups of the apple juice and leave to soak for 2 hours.

2 Bring the apple juice to the boil, reduce the heat and simmer for 10 minutes, then leave to cool. Using a slotted spoon, lift out one-quarter of the dates, chop roughly and set aside.

3 Purée the remaining dates in a food processor or blender. Add the cinnamon and process with enough of the apple juice to make a smooth paste.

4 Add the cubes of beancurd (tofu), a few at a time, processing after each addition. Add the remaining apple juice and the soya milk.

5 **By hand:** Pour the mixture into a plastic tub or similar freezerproof container and freeze for 4 hours, beating once with a fork, electric mixer or in a food processor to break up the ice crystals. After this time, beat again with a fork to ensure a smooth texture.

Using an ice cream maker: Churn the mixture until very thick, but not thick enough to scoop. Scrape into a plastic tub.

6 Add most of the remaining dates to the mixture and stir to combine. Freeze for 2–3 hours until firm.

7 Scoop the ice cream into dessert glasses, decorate with the remaining chopped dates and serve immediately.

— NUTRITION NOTES —	
Per portion:	
Energy	188kcals/797kJ
Protein	7.8g
Fat, total	3.9g
saturated fat	0.5g
Carbohydrate	32.5g
of which sugars	32.2g
Fibre	0.9g

— HEALTH BENEFITS —
Isoflavones found in beancurd (tofu) can help to ease menopausal symptoms.

Poached Winter Fruits

The fruits in this recipe provide a rich supply of valuable age-defying antioxidants that will benefit any anti-ageing diet. Served hot, the dish will also help to warm the body during the cold winter months.

INGREDIENTS

Serves 6
475ml/16fl oz/2 cups freshly
  squeezed orange juice
finely grated rind and juice of 1 orange
120ml/4fl oz/½ cup red wine
45ml/3 tbsp clear honey
1 cinnamon stick, broken
  in half
4 cloves
4 cardamom pods, split
2 pears, such as Comice or William,
  peeled, cored and halved
8 ready-to-eat dried figs
12 ready-to-eat dried
  unsulphured apricots
2 eating apples, peeled, cored and
  thickly sliced

1 Pour the orange juice into a large, heavy pan and add half the orange rind, the red wine, honey, cinnamon stick, cloves and cardamom pods.

2 Bring the orange juice and spices to the boil, then reduce the heat and simmer gently for about 2 minutes, stirring occasionally.

3 Add the halved pears and dried figs and apricots to the pan and cook, covered, for 25 minutes, turning the fruit over occasionally with a wooden spoon. Add the sliced apples and cook for a further 12–15 minutes until the fruit is tender and juicy.

--- HEALTH BENEFITS ---

The combination of fresh and dried fruit provides a healthy dose of anti-ageing vitamins and minerals, including vitamin C, betacarotene, potassium and iron.

4 Remove the fruit from the pan with a slotted spoon and place them in a bowl. Remove the spices from the juice and discard. Boil the juices over a high heat until reduced and syrupy, then pour over the fruit. Serve decorated with the remaining orange rind, if wished.

--- NUTRITION NOTES ---

Per portion:
Energy	344kcals/1465kJ
Protein	5.4g
Fat, total	1.9g
saturated fat	0g
Carbohydrate	81.4g
of which sugars	81.4g
Fibre	10.8g

Fruit Platter with Cinnamon and Ginger

Pomegranates contain healing plant chemicals that will zap away viruses in a matter of seconds. Use other deep-coloured exotic fruit and don't be surprised if you end up liking this dessert more than you thought you would.

INGREDIENTS

Serves 6
2 papayas
1 pineapple
1 small melon
juice of 2 limes
2 pomegranates
ground cinnamon and ginger,
    to taste
sprigs of mint, to decorate (optional)

1 Peel the papayas, cut them in half, and then into thin wedges. Peel the pineapple. Remove the core and any remaining "eyes", then cut the flesh lengthways into thin wedges. Halve the melon and remove the seeds from the middle. Cut it into thin wedges and remove the skin.

2 Arrange the papaya, pineapple and melon slices on six individual plates and sprinkle with lime juice. Cut the pomegranates in half and scoop out the seeds, discarding any pith.

3 Scatter the seeds over the prepared fruit and serve, sprinkled with a little ground cinnamon and ginger to taste. Scatter over a few sprigs of fresh mint if you like.

HEALTH BENEFITS

Orange-fleshed fruits such as papaya are rich in the useful antioxidant nutrient betacarotene. Limes and pineapple offer good supplies of antioxidant vitamin C, while melons are believed to stimulate the kidneys, helping them to work more efficiently and detoxify the body.

NUTRITION NOTES

Per portion:

Energy	98kcals/416kJ
Protein	1.3g
Fat, total	0.4g
saturated fat	0g
Carbohydrate	23.6g
of which sugars	23.6g
Fibre	3.8g

Fresh Fruit Salad

Cooking fruits can destroy their nutrients so this fresh fruit salad is perfect if you want to make the most of your ingredients.

INGREDIENTS

Serves 6
2 peaches
2 eating apples
2 oranges
16–20 strawberries
30ml/2 tbsp lemon juice
15–30ml/1–2 tbsp orange flower water
a few fresh mint leaves, to decorate

1 Blanch the peaches for 1 minute in boiling water, then peel away the skin and cut the flesh into thick slices. Discard the stone (pit).

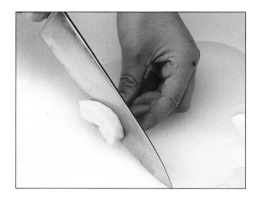

2 Peel and core the apples and cut into thin slices. Peel the oranges with a sharp knife, removing all the pith, and segment them, catching any juice in a bowl.

3 Hull the strawberries and halve or quarter if large. Place all the fruit in a large serving bowl.

4 Blend together the lemon juice, orange flower water and any orange juice you managed to catch when segmenting the oranges.

5 Pour the fruit juice mixture over the salad and toss lightly to combine. Serve decorated with a few fresh mint leaves.

— NUTRITION NOTES —	
Per portion:	
Energy	40kcals/169kJ
Protein	1g
Fat, total	0.1g
saturated fat	0g
Carbohydrate	9.2g
of which sugars	9.2g
Fibre	1.7g

Dried Fruit Salad with Summer Berries

Great for the eyes, this dried fruit salad contains plentiful supplies of antioxidants, which are thought to reduce the risk of cataracts and macular degeneration later in life, and the eye-protecting nutrients lutein and zeaxanthin.

INGREDIENTS

Serves 4
115g/4oz/½ cup ready-to-eat
  dried apricots
115g/4oz/½ cup ready-to-eat
  dried peaches
1 pear
1 apple
1 orange
115g/4oz/⅔ cup mixed raspberries
  and blackberries
1 cinnamon stick
30ml/2 tbsp clear honey
30ml/2 tbsp lemon juice

1 Soak the dried apricots and peaches in water for 1–2 hours until plump and juicy, then drain and halve or quarter, using a sharp knife.

2 Peel and core the pear and apple and cut into cubes. Peel the orange with a sharp knife, removing all the white pith, and cut into wedges. Place all the fruit in a large pan with the raspberries and blackberries.

3 Add 550ml/18fl oz/2½ cups water, the cinnamon and clear honey.

4 Bring to the boil, then cover the pan and allow to simmer very gently for 10–12 minutes, until the fruit is just tender, stirring occasionally.

5 Remove the pan from the heat and stir in the lemon juice. Allow to cool, then pour into a serving bowl and chill for 1–2 hours before serving.

— NUTRITION NOTES —	
Per portion:	
Energy	124kcals/532kJ
Protein	3g
Fat, total	0.5g
saturated fat	0g
Carbohydrate	28.8g
of which sugars	28.8g
Fibre	5.7g

Blueberry and Orange Crêpe Baskets

The blueberries in this appetizing dish are full of lutein, which is thought to protect the eyes.

INGREDIENTS

Serves 4
150g/5oz/1¼ cups plain
   (all-purpose) flour
pinch of salt
2 egg whites
200ml/7fl oz/scant 1 cup
   skimmed milk
150ml/¼ pint/⅔ cup orange juice

For the filling
4 medium-size oranges
225g/8oz/2 cups blueberries

1 Preheat the oven to 200°C/400°F/ Gas 6. To make the crêpes, sift the flour and salt into a bowl. Make a well in the centre of the flour and add the egg whites, milk and orange juice. Whisk hard, until all the liquid has been incorporated and the batter is smooth and bubbly.

2 Lightly grease a heavy or non-stick pancake pan and heat it until it is very hot. Pour in just enough batter to cover the base of the pan, swirling it to cover the base evenly.

3 Cook until the pancake has set and is golden, and then turn it to cook the other side.

4 Remove the cooked pancake from the pan and place on a sheet of absorbent kitchen paper, then cook the remaining batter, to make a further seven pancakes.

5 Place eight small ovenproof bowls or moulds on a baking sheet and arrange the pancakes over these. Bake in the oven for about 10 minutes, until they are crisp and set into shape. Lift the crêpes off the moulds.

6 Pare a thin piece of orange rind from one orange and cut it into fine strips. Blanch the strips in boiling water for 30 seconds, rinse in cold water and set aside. Cut all the peel and white pith from all the oranges.

7 Divide the oranges into segments, catching the juice. Combine with the blueberries and warm the mixture gently. Spoon into the baskets and scatter the shreds of rind over the top. These baskets are delicious served with yogurt or light crème fraîche.

---- COOK'S TIP ----

Don't fill the pancake baskets until you're ready to serve them, because they will absorb the fruit juice and begin to soften.

---- NUTRITION NOTES ----

Per portion:

Energy	159kcals/678kJ
Protein	6g
Fat, total	0.5g
saturated fat	0.1g
Carbohydrate	34.8g
of which sugars	15.8g
Fibre	4g

Strawberry Rose-petal Pashka

This version of a traditional Russian dessert is brimming with the goodness of lutein-rich strawberries. The addition of rose water gives the dish an extra aroma.

INGREDIENTS

Serves 4
350g/12oz/1½ cups cottage cheese
175ml/6fl oz/¾ cup low-fat
   natural yogurt
30ml/2 tbsp clear honey
2.5ml/½ tsp rose water
275g/10oz/2½ cups strawberries
handful of scented pink rose petals,
   to decorate

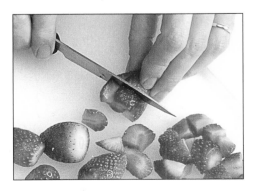

1 Strain any free liquid from the cottage cheese and tip the cheese into a strainer. Use a wooden spoon to rub it through the strainer into a bowl.

2 Stir the yogurt, honey and rose water into the cheese.

3 Roughly chop about half the strawberries and stir them into the cheese mixture.

4 Line an unused, clean flowerpot or a strainer with fine muslin and tip in the cottage cheese and strawberry mixture. Leave the mixture to drain over a bowl for several hours or overnight if there is time.

5 Invert the flowerpot or strainer on to a serving plate, turn out the pashka and remove the muslin.

6 Decorate the pashka with the reserved strawberries and pink rose petals. Serve chilled.

--- NUTRITION NOTES ---

Per portion:

Energy	150kcals/634kJ
Protein	14.9g
Fat, total	3.8g
saturated fat	2.3g
Carbohydrate	15g
of which sugars	15g
Fibre	0.8g

Pineapple and Cinnamon Drop Scones

A traditional English afternoon tea needn't be a nightmare for anyone who is watching their cholesterol. These drop scones contain very little fat.

INGREDIENTS

Makes 24
225g/8oz/2 cups self-raising (self-rising) wholemeal (whole-wheat) flour
5ml/1 tsp ground cinnamon
1 egg
300ml/½ pint/1¼ cups pineapple juice
75g/3oz/½ cup semi-dried pineapple, chopped

1 Preheat a griddle, heavy frying pan or an electric frying pan. Put the wholemeal flour in a mixing bowl. Add the cinnamon and make a well in the centre. Add the egg with half of the pineapple juice.

2 Gradually incorporate the flour to make a smooth batter. Beat in the remaining pineapple juice with the chopped semi-dried pineapple.

3 Lightly grease the heated griddle or pan. Drop tablespoons of the pineapple batter on to the surface, leaving them until they bubble on top and the bubbles begin to burst.

4 Carefully turn the drop scones over with a palette knife (metal spatula) and cook until the underside is golden brown. Pat dry with kitchen paper and continue to cook in successive batches.

NUTRITION NOTES

Per portion:	
Energy	40kcals/168kJ
Protein	1.6g
Fat, total	0.5g
saturated fat	0.1g
Carbohydrate	7.8g
of which sugars	1.8g
Fibre	0g

Chewy Fruit Muesli Slice

Oaty muesli is an excellent anti-ageing food, so it makes a great ingredient in these chewy slices. As well as adding flavour, the dried apricots and apples provide an extra boost of the valuable antioxidant vitamin E.

INGREDIENTS

Makes 8

75g/3oz/½ cup ready-to-eat dried apricots, chopped
1 eating apple, cored and grated
150g/5oz/1¼ cups Swiss-style muesli
150ml/¼ pint/⅔ cup apple juice
15g/½oz/1 tbsp soft butter

1 Preheat the oven to 190°C/375°F/ Gas 5. Place all the ingredients together in a large bowl and mix well with a wooden spoon until combined.

2 Press the mixture into a 20cm/8in non-stick sandwich tin (pan) with the back of a wooden spoon and bake for 35–40 minutes, until lightly browned and firm.

3 Using a sharp knife, mark the fruit muesli slice into eight equal-size wedges while it is still hot. Leave to cool in the tin (pan).

4 When the muesli slice has cooled, break into pieces and serve, or store in an airtight container.

NUTRITION NOTES	
Per portion:	
Energy	107kcals/452kJ
Protein	2.3g
Fat, total	2.7g
saturated fat	1.2g
Carbohydrate	19.6g
of which sugars	10.9g
Fibre	1.9g

Spiced Apple Cake

This apple cake contains very little saturated fat, making it a good cake for an anti-ageing diet.

INGREDIENTS

Serves 8

225g/8oz/2 cups self-raising (self-rising) wholemeal (whole-wheat) flour
5ml/1 tsp baking powder
10ml/2 tsp ground cinnamon
175g/6oz/1 cup chopped dates
75g/3oz/½ cup light muscovado (molasses) sugar
15ml/1 tbsp pear and apple spread
120ml/4fl oz/½ cup apple juice
2 eggs
90ml/6 tbsp sunflower oil
2 eating apples, cored and grated
15ml/1 tbsp chopped walnuts

1 Preheat the oven to 180°C/350°F/ Gas 4. Grease and line a deep, round 20cm/8in cake tin (pan).

2 Sift the wholemeal flour, baking powder and cinnamon into a mixing bowl, then add the dates and mix into the dry ingredients. Make a well in the centre.

3 Mix the sugar with the pear and apple spread in a small bowl. Gradually stir in the apple juice. Add to the dry ingredients with the eggs, oil and apples. Mix thoroughly.

4 Spoon the mixture into the cake tin (pan), sprinkle with walnuts and bake for 60 minutes or until a skewer comes out clean. Transfer to a rack, remove the paper and leave to cool.

COOK'S TIP

Leave the apple peel on as the skin adds extra fibre and softens on cooking.

NUTRITION NOTES

Per portion:

Energy	294kcals/1239kJ
Protein	6.3g
Fat, total	11.7g
saturated fat	1.6g
Carbohydrate	43.6g
of which sugars	26.2g
Fibre	3.6g

Information File

Useful Addresses

Australia
Australian Cancer Society
PO Box 4708
Sydney NSW 2001
Tel: (02) 2267 1944

Diabetes Australia
National Office
5–7 Phipps Place
Deakin ACT 2615
Tel: 1 (800) 640 862

Canada
Canadian Cancer Society
10 Alcorn Avenue
Toronto
Ontario M4V 3B1
Tel: (001) 416 293 7422

Canadian Diabetic Association
15 Toronto Street
Suite 800
Toronto
Ontario M5C 2E3
Tel: (001) 416 363 3373

New Zealand
**Cancer Society of
New Zealand**
PO Box 1724
Auckland
Tel: (09) 524 2628

South Africa
Diabetes Association
PO Box 1715
Saxonwold 21342
Tel: (011) 788 4595

United Kingdom
Arthritis Research Campaign
41 Eagle Street
London WC1R 4AR
Tel: 01246 558033

Arthritic Association
Suite 2, Hyde Gardens
Eastbourne
East Sussex BN21 4PN
Tel: 01323 416550

**Bristol Cancer Help
Centre**
Grove House
Cornwallis Grove
Clifton
Bristol BS8 4PG
Tel: 0117 980 9505

**British Diabetic
Association**
10 Queen Anne's Street
London W1M 0BD
Tel: 020 7323 1531

British Heart Foundation
14 Fitzhardinge Street
London W1H 4DH
Tel: 020 7935 0185

**British Nutrition
Foundation**
High Holborn House
52–54 High Holborn
London WC1V 6RQ
Tel: 020 7404 6504

**Institute for Complementary
Medicine**
PO Box 194
London SE16 1QZ
Tel: 020 7237 5165

**Institute for Optimum
Nutrition**
Blades Court
Deodar Road
London SW15 2NU
Tel: 020 8877 9993

**National Association of
Health Stores**
Wayside Cottage
Cuckoo Corner
Urchfont
Devizes SN10 4RA
Tel: 01380 840133

**The National Osteoporosis
Society**
PO Box 10
Bath BA3 3YB
Tel: 01761 471 771

**Royal Society for the
Promotion of Health**
38a St George's Drive
London SW1V 4BH
Tel: 020 7630 0121

United States
**The American Diabetes
Association**
1660 Duke Street
Alexandria, VA 22314
Tel: (800) 232-3472

**The American Dietetic
Association**
216 West Jackson Boulevard
Chicago, IL 60606
Tel: (312) 899-0040
www.eatright.org

**American Health and
Nutrition Inc.**
3990 Varsity Drive
Ann Arbor, MI 48108
Tel: (734) 677-5570
www.organictrading.com

**American Heart
Association**
National Center
7272 Greenville Avenue
Dallas, TX 75231
Tel: (800) 242-8721
www.americanheart.org

**American Society for
Nutritional Sciences**
9650 Rockville Pike
Bethesda, MD 20814
Tel: (301) 530-7050

The Arthritis Foundation
1330 West Peachtree Street
Atlanta, GA 30309
Tel: (800) 283-7800
www.arthritis.org

**Center for Food Safety &
Applied Nutrition**
200 C Street SW
Washington, DC 20204
www.cfsan.fda.gov

**Food and Nutrition
Information Center**
National Agricultural Library
Room 304
10301 Baltimore Avenue
Beltsville, MD 20705
Tel: (301) 504-5719
www.nal.usda.gov/fnic

**National Center for
Complementary and
Alternative Medicine**
P.O. Box 8218
Silver Springs, MD 20907
Tel: (888) 644-6226
www.nccam.nih.gov

**National Institute of Arthritis
and Musculoskeletal and
Skin Diseases**
National Institute of Health
Bethesda, MD 20892
Tel: (301) 496-8188
www.nih.gov/niams

**National Institute on
Aging**
Building 31, Room 5C27
31 Center Drive, MSC 2292
Bethesda, MD 20892
Tel: (301) 496-1752
www.nih.gov/nia

**National Osteoporosis
Foundation**
1232 22nd Street NW
Washington, DC 20037
Tel: (202) 223-2226
www.nof.org

Index

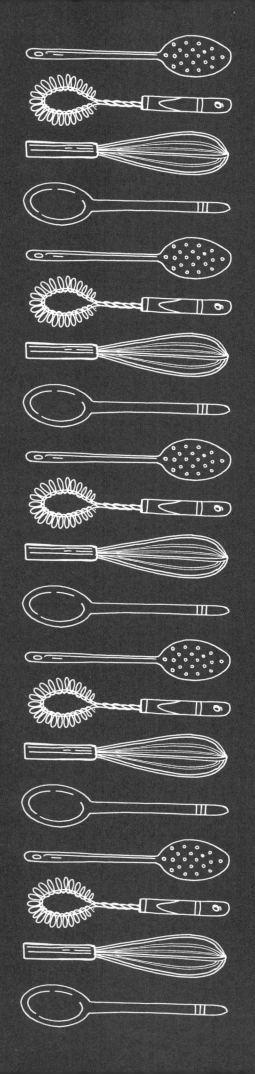